THE HOMERIC CENTONES

AND

THE ACTS OF PILATE

THE HOMERIC CENTONES

AND

THE ACTS OF PILATE

BY

J. RENDEL HARRIS,

UNIVERSITY LECTURER IN PALÆOGRAPHY
AND FELLOW OF CLARE COLLEGE, CAMBRIDGE.

WIPF & STOCK · Eugene, Oregon

Wipf and Stock Publishers
199 W 8th Ave, Suite 3
Eugene, OR 97401

The Homeric Centones and the Acts of the Pilate
By Harris, J. Rendel
Softcover ISBN-13: 978-1-7252-7967-4
Publication date 5/1/2020
Previously published by CJ Clay and Sons, 1898

PREFACE.

THE notes which are contained in the following pages have been lying by me for several years, in the hope that I might find it possible to complete and correct the investigation by a study of the MSS. involved. But no such opportunity as I desired has presented itself, and it has occurred to me that the publication of this imperfect dissertation might enable some other student to pursue more successfully an enquiry, my own share in which I can only describe as preliminary and tentative. I am much indebted to Mr Conybeare and Mr McEvoy for their kindness in reading the proof-sheets.

CONTENTS.

CHAPTER I.
Early Versifications of the Scriptures . . . . . . 1—18

CHAPTER II.
Early Editions of the Centones and traces of their use by Milton 19—33

CHAPTER III.
Authorship and Date of the Homeric Centones . . . . 34—42

CHAPTER IV.
Literary Parallelism between the Homeric Centones and the Acts of Pilate . . . . 43—50

CHAPTER V.
Homeric Structure of the Acts of Pilate . . . . . 51—58

CHAPTER VI.
Homeric Structure of the Descensus ad Inferos . . . . 59—67

CHAPTER VII.
Justin Martyr and the Acta Pilati . . . . 68—75

CHAPTER VIII.
Directions for Further Enquiry . . . . 76—83

CHAPTER I.

ON THE EARLY VERSIFICATIONS OF THE SCRIPTURES.

THE object of the present tract is the critical examination of a metrical form of the Scriptures which was current in very early times, and underwent a good deal of editing in the sixteenth and seventeenth centuries, though it has since been almost lost sight of; and to point out the reflex influence which this pseudo-poetry exercised upon the literature and the legends of the Christian Church. I refer, as my title shews, to the Homeric versifications which pass under the name of *Centones, Homero-centrones,* or *Homero-centra,* in which, by a skilful adaptation and piecing together of verses and half-verses of Homer, with a few necessary modifications, the narrative of the Gospels was transferred from its natural simplicity into a ridiculous mimicry of the reverberating music of the Greek epic, which, no doubt, pleased the learned by its ingenuity and deceived the unlearned by its affected stateliness[1].

The popularity of these compositions is not confined to any particular age, and they are as much in demand in the sixteenth century as in the second.

Some idea of the interest which has been taken in the Homeric Centones since the invention of printing may be gathered from the fact that they were published from the Aldine press as early as A.D. 1504, two years before the appearance of the second

[1] The proper name for such compositions is κέντρωνες, which passed into the Latin as *centones*. At all events Tertullian and Jerome know them as *Homero-centones, Virgilio-centones*. That the vulgar were really deceived by such compositions appears from a specimen given by Irenaeus, who remarks, Τίς οὐκ ἂν τῶν ἀπανούργων συναρπαγείη ὑπὸ τῶν ἐπῶν τούτων καὶ νομίσειεν οὕτως αὐτὰ ῞Ομηρον ἐπὶ ταύτης τῆς ὑποθέσεως πεποιηκέναι; ὁ δ' ἔμπειρος τῆς Ὁμηρικῆς ὑποθέσεως ἐπιγνώσεται μὲν τὰ ἔπη, τὴν δ' ὑπόθεσιν οὐκ ἐπιγνώσεται (ed. Mass. p. 46).

edition of Homer, and within fourteen years of the *editio princeps*[1]; and that the interest was well sustained appears from the rapid succession of editions, of which no less than five were produced between A.D. 1502 and A.D. 1609, the last of which is remarkable on account of its being a school-book for use in the Jesuit order[2]! It is difficult to estimate the meaning of this rapid sequence of editions; it cannot be due to the critical value of the Centones in regard to the text of Homer himself, for it will be difficult to extract any philology or textual interpretation from the confused mass of quotations which make up the story; nor can it be that any theological light was thought to be cast by them on the problems of the early Christian faith and tradition; for, although we shall shew that they do furnish abundant and important evidence on certain obscure religious and literary phenomena, there is not the least reason for supposing that any of the conclusions to which we shall presently direct our readers were suspected by those who in the sixteenth and seventeenth centuries tortured themselves in reading the tortured Gospel. Some explanation may be found in the fact that the Centones were an attempt at Christianizing Homer, especially in the interests of young scholars: the nude pagan statue needed drapery which early Homeric editors found ready to their hand in the rag-bag of the Centonists. That this consideration really had some weight may be seen from the prefatory matter in the Aldine edition as well as from the patronage of the Jesuits. Aldus says expressly that he designed his edition for the use of schools, in order that children of tender age might not be corrupted by heathen poetry; and he intimates that certain evilly-disposed persons shewed special spite against the production of the work, which they tried in every way to hinder. Moreover, as we shall see presently, he arranged his text and Latin translation in such a manner that the Greek and Latin could be detached and bound up separately, which again suggests the use of schools. As for the Jesuits, who are amongst

---

[1] The *editio princeps* of Homer is the Florence edition of 1488, under the editorial care of Demetrius Chalcondylas of Athens and Demetrius of Crete. The second is the Aldine edition of 1504. A discussion of the early editions of the Centones will be found *infra*, c. 2.

[2] A copy in my possession is actually marked "Collegii Societ. Jesu Ingolstadii anno 1609." One feels like saying of Homer what the Scriptures do of Samson, "Duxerunt Gazam vinctum catenis et clausum in carcere molere fecerunt," Judg. xvi. 21.

the first and foremost in the history of educational progress, they did not actually expel Homer; the *Ratio Studiorum* shews that a place was found for him in the curriculum, which seems not to have been the case with Euripides and Sophocles. Probably the younger students read the Centones, and the older the complete poet[1].

But probably the right way to appreciate the literary fondness for the biblical Homeric Cento, at all events in early times, is to regard it as a part of a much wider series of phenomena; we may discuss it as a single case of the multiform witchcraft of Homer over the human race, or we may regard the Centones as a single link in the long chain of attempts at versification of the Hebrew and Christian Scriptures; or, combining the two points of view, we may regard the verses as the most striking attempt ever made to translate one Bible into the language of another.

We are not concerned in the present study with the influence of Homer upon literature generally, though it is impossible to explain some of the phenomena which occur in Hellenistic and later Greek without some appreciation of his wonderful dominance. Apart from the question of Biblical versifications and adaptations, we need a proper feeling of his just and undying supremacy in the world of letters—if indeed it be possible in the present day to obtain such an adequate estimate—and to recall the time when everyone knew the *Iliad* and *Odyssey*, or at all events the more striking portions of them, and when almost everyone could quote them. To take an instance, who would ever have thought of commencing a dialogue between a Christian and a Jew in the second century by a quotation from Homer? yet we find that Justin opens his discourse with Trypho by the playful quotation: Τίς δὲ σύ ἐσσι, φέριστε, βροτῶν; οὕτως προσπαίζων αὐτῷ ἔλεγον· nor is there any reason to suppose that the source of the quotation would have been obscure to Trypho, who confesses to Justin that he takes a great interest in the Socratic philosophy[2]. Those were days when even the Rabbis[3] had Homer under their pillows. Who,

[1] Γάλα ἐπότισα ὑμᾶς: and very sour milk!

[2] If it should turn out, which I do not expect, that Trypho in the dialogue is a mere imaginary lay-figure, we should simply say that Justin has borrowed an artistic touch for his verbal conflict from the meeting of Glaucus and Diomed on the plains of Troy. But it seems to me in every way likely that we have here the summary of a real discourse, though perhaps based on a conventional method.

[3] As Rabbi Akiba; see T. J. Sanh. 28ᵃ.

again, would have expected that a Jewish proselyte would, in translating the Hebrew Scriptures into Greek, have gone out of his way to employ Homeric diction? Yet it is demonstrable that Aquila of Pontus did this; nor is it easy to avoid the double conclusion (i) that Homer was a part of the common-school education in Pontus, (ii) that the Rabbinical protests against Greek learning were, at least in the second century, to a great extent mere *fulmina bruta*[1]. Or to take an instance which shews the persistence as well as the seriousness of Homeric studies among the early Christians, who would have expected that a Christian martyr in the year 303 would have secured his decapitation by meeting the demand to make a libation to the emperors with the words,

Οὐκ ἀγαθὸν πολυκοιρανίη, εἶς κοίρανος ἔστω,
Εἶς βασιλεύς
(*Il.* B. 204; Euseb. *Mart. Patl.* c. 1)?

We can see from this instance how near the quotation was to words that are canonically holy[2].

The influence of Homer upon the early Jewish and Christian writers is not confined to professedly philosophic writers like Justin, nor to perverts like Aquila. It is patent in the New Testament itself, and especially in the Apocalypse. For example, when St John wrote the vision of the dragon which attempts to destroy the Man-Child that is born into the world, he had in his mind the vision of Calchas in the second book of the *Iliad*, who narrates the devouring of a brood of nestlings and their mother by a fiery-red dragon. We have only to compare the language

καὶ σημεῖον μέγα ὤφθη ἐν τῷ οὐρανῷ...καὶ ἰδοὺ δράκων μέγας πυρρός... (Apoc. xii. 1, 3)

with the verse of Homer (*Il.* B. 308),

Ἔνθ' ἐφάνη μέγα σῆμα· δράκων ἐπὶ νῶτα δαφοινός,

and we see at once that the one passage is the literary origin of the other. The object of the dragon is to devour the brood, but

---

[1] A recent writer in the *Jewish Quarterly Review* saves the literary reputation of the Rabbis by sacrificing their moral character; the books against which a crusade was ordered were not the works of Homer but βιβλία ἱμέρου, presumably erotic writings. To prove that Homer was not prohibited he gets rid of the evidence that he was read.

[2] The same quotation used theologically in Justin, *Cohort.* 17.

this is not permitted in the vision in the Apocalypse, where both Mother and Child escape. It is interesting to observe that in the Apocalyptic writer's mind, the mother is really a bird, for when the dragon proceeds to persecute her, she takes to herself the two wings of a great eagle, and flies into the desert. Moreover she has a whole brood of nestlings, and not merely the single Man-Child; for the writer tells us that the dragon proceeded to make war with the remnant of her seed, those, namely, who keep the commands of God and the testimony of Jesus[1].

A similar Homeric touch occurs in c. ix. 1, where a mighty angel descends from heaven, cloud-robed and rainbow-crowned. The writer had Iris, the messenger of the gods, in his mind, and he avoided the pagan conception by turning his Iris into an ornament of the descending angel.

Other traces of Homeric influence may be found in the Apocalypse; we do not attempt to deal with the subject exhaustively, but only to impress the sense of the ubiquity of Homer in all early literature[2].

Why should we doubt that the *Odyssey* penetrated into Palestine when we know from the story of Ulysses Mac Laertes that it reached Ireland[3]? And if Dionysius of Halicarnassus was right in comparing the influence of Homer to the might of his own "ocean stream, from which flow all other rivers and seas and all fountains of waters[4]," by what reason is the Jordan or the

---

[1] Ephrem Syrus uses the passage of the Apocalypse to describe the Innocents in a Hymn on the Nativity (Lamy, II. 471):

> Ingemuerunt columbae in Bethlehem,
> Quod serpens earum proles destruxisset;
> Aquila in Aegyptum se contulit,
> Ut illuc descendens acciperet promissiones.

And in our own times Mr Gore has argued that a knowledge of the infancy sections in Matthew is implied in the Apocalypse. See *Dissertations*, p. 10.

[2] What occurs in the Apocalypse occurs also, perhaps, in the Lucan writings; and indeed it would be strange if an author, like St Luke, who has been credited with an acquaintance with Dioscorides, should shew no influence of mightier models of style and speech. In his recent work on the *Philology of the Gospels* Dr Blass has argued that the expression ἐπέκειλαν τὴν ναῦν in Acts xxvii. 41 is Homeric (cf. *Odyssey*, IX. 148, 546). And there is another important passage to be discussed in the same connexion to which we may return later.

[3] The Irish text will be found translated by Kuno Meyer: see *Merugud Uilix Maicc Leirtis* (London, Nutt, 1886).

[4] *Il.* Φ. 195.

sea of Galilee exiled from this all-embracing stream, and its all-supplying flow[1]?

We may, indeed, grant that Jewish literature has become a shrunken stream discharging itself into a Dead Sea of Talmudical precepts and legends, but the evidence of the stratification of the literature shews that, like the sacred river itself, it was in former days no such pigmy channel, but a mighty flood in touch with the outmost main. We might reasonably doubt whether the Jews would ever have given so much to the thought and religion of the outside world, if we were required to assume that they had taken nothing therefrom. Admitting then the extent of Homer's influence, which we can trace from the Borysthenes[2] to the Shannon, and from Pontus to Massilia[3], and reminding ourselves of a fact of which all ancient literature furnishes so abundant proofs, that there never was an author so paraphrased, parodied, centonized and generally imitated as Homer, let us now turn and look at the Centones from the other point of view: let us consider them as a successful attempt at the verse-translation of the Scriptures.

As soon as we begin to think of the versification of the Scriptures we realize that we are dealing again with no isolated phenomenon. The Centones are only one of a series of similar efforts, in which the resources of Greek lyric, epic, and tragedy, were made to contribute to the presentation of the Biblical story and of Jewish and Christian doctrine.

We recall, for example, the *Christus Patiens*, long supposed to be a work of Gregory of Nazianzus, which tells the Gospel in language borrowed from six plays of Euripides, viz., Medea, Orestes, Bacchae, Hippolytus, Troades, and Rhesus; the piece is valuable, not so much for its presentation of the historical foundations of the faith, as for the criticism of the incorporated dramas of Euripides, especially the Rhesus[4].

[1] Theodore of Tarsus, who had such influence in settling the religion of the English, carried a copy of Homer with him wherever he travelled. An evangelist with Homer up his sleeve would be a good hieroglyphic to represent a number of developments in the faith and practice of the Church.

[2] Dion Cassius tells us of the passion of the Borysthenitae for Homer.

[3] Massilia had the honour of producing one of the standard texts of Homer.

[4] Mrs Browning in her essay on the Greek Christian poets follows a conjecture which ascribes this composition to Apollinarius, mainly because it is not good enough to be the work of Gregory; and makes a happy translation of the opening verses

Then we have the Psalms in epic form from the hand of Apollinarius, a striking figure in the procession, which Lord Byron alliterating reviles, of those who

> "boldly pilfer from the Pentateuch,
> And undisturbed by conscientious qualms
> Pervert the Prophets and purloin the Psalms."

Another poem in similar metre is Nonnus' famous paraphrase of the Gospel of St John, which, as the critical apparatus of Tischendorf's New Testament will shew, is not destitute of value in the determination of the sacred text.

Over against these writers of Greek verse and others, their contemporaries, whose works have not survived, we have a Latin company, embracing such writers as Juvencus, the author of the Evangelical History, Cyprian the author of the Latin Heptateuch, Proba Faltonia, who imitated the Homer Centones in the language of Virgil, and a number of others.

It will be seen that there was a steady stream of Biblical versification flowing in the early centuries of the Christian era.

Not only is this the case, but, what is more remarkable, we find traces of a similar stream in the centuries which immediately precede the Christian era. Not a single one of these works has come down to us, but there are sufficient fragments preserved to give us a very good idea of the literary activity of the time.

by way of comparison with the *Medea* of Euripides, which they imitate. "The tragedy is, in fact, a specimen of Centoism, which is the adaptation of the phraseology of one work to the construction of another; and we have only to glance at it to perceive the *Medea* of Euripides, dislocated into the *Christus Patiens*. Instead of the ancient opening,

> 'Oh, would ship Argo had not sailed away
> To Colchos by the rough Symplegades!
> Nor ever had been felled, in Pelion's grove,
> The pine, hewn for her side! So she, my queen,
> Medea had not touched this fatal shore,
> Soul-struck by love of Jason!'

Apollinarius (!) opens it thus:

> 'Oh, would the serpent had not glode along
> To Eden's garden-land—nor ever had
> The crafty dragon planted in that grove
> A slimy snare! So she, rib-born of man,
> The wretched misled mother of our race,
> Had dared not to dare on beyond worst daring,
> Soul-struck by love of—apples!'"

We know of three poets who occupied themselves with the versification of the Old Testament, to say nothing of those who wrote under the literary disguise of the Sibyl. These three are Philo, the epic poet, who writes the history of the city of Jerusalem; Theodotus, who writes the story of Shechem as given in the book of Genesis; and Ezekiel, who dramatized the story of the Exodus after the manner of a Greek play. Our knowledge of all these writers is ultimately derived from the lost collections of Alexander Polyhistor, though the actual quotations and references occur in the pages of Josephus, Clement of Alexandria, and Eusebius[1].

It is difficult to place any of these writers later than the second century before the Christian era. But if this be the case, their evidence becomes particularly weighty in questions relating to the religion and education of that time, and the prominence of the Greek language and literature amongst the Jews. For example, the tragedy of Ezekiel, which, to judge from the name, is certainly the work of a Jew, is based not on the Hebrew text of Exodus, but on the Septuagint. A very few verses placed side by side with the account in Exodus will shew this[2]. Closer

---

[1] The proof of the indebtedness of these writers to Alexander Polyhistor is not difficult. Eusebius in his *Praeparatio Evangelica*, lib. ix., makes copious extracts from Polyhistor, and amongst these extracts are the fragments of Theodotus' poem on Shechem, as quoted by Polyhistor. Later on in the same book, but still quoting Polyhistor, he gives extracts from Ezekiel's drama of the Exodus. But a large part of the very same extracts are found quoted by Clement in the *Stromateis*, who follows closely the Eusebian text—and in one case even drops the connecting formula of Polyhistor (μεθ' ἕτερα ἐπιλέγει) which we find in Eusebius, so as to take two consecutive extracts in Eusebius continuously. It is clear, then, that Clement is working on the same collection of extracts, but with less regard to the continuity of the verses.

The epic poet Philo is referred to by Josephus, Clement and Eusebius: from the fact that Josephus and Clement quote him along with the historians Demetrius and Eupolemus, and in the same order (Demetrius, Philo and Eupolemus), it is plain that they are working on a common collection of excerpts from these writers, and this collection must be the work of Alexander Polyhistor, from which Eusebius takes his extracts. Cf. Freudenthal, *Alexander Polyhistor*, p. 12.

[2] Moses describes his exposure in the ark of bulrushes as follows:

οὐ λαθοῦσα δὲ
ὑπεξέθηκε, κόσμον ἀμφιθεῖσά μοι,
παρ' ἄκρα ποταμοῦ, λάσιον, εἰς ἕλος δασύ.
Μαριὰμ δ' ἀδελφή μου κατώπτευεν πέλας·
κἄπειτα θυγάτηρ βασιλέως ἅβραις ὁμοῦ
κατῆλθε λουτροῖς χρῶτα φαιδρῦναι νέον.

examination shews that the acquaintance with the Septuagint is more than would be expected from a mere versifier, working on a text. Further the writer's acquaintance with Greek literature is not limited to the Greek Bible, nor to a tragic poet or two; he knew his Homer also: the concluding verses of Eusebius's extract could never have been written by anyone whose mind was not saturated with Homeric language and ideas [1].

πάντα γὰρ τὰ πτῆν᾽ ὁμοῦ
ὄπισθεν αὐτοῦ δειλιῶντ᾽ ἐπέσσυτο,
αὐτὸς δὲ πρόσθεν, ταῦρος ὡς γαυρούμενος
ἔβαινε κραιπνὸν βῆμα βαστάζων ποδός.

How thoroughly Homeric this, though not written in the metre of the epic, both in thought and language. We recognise the comparison of the marching Greeks to a flight of birds (*Il.* B. 459), of Agamemnon to a βοῦς ταῦρος (*Il.* B. 480), while the last line echoes the continual ποσὶ κραιπνοῖσι of the *Iliad*.

Compare also the verse which describes the onslaught of the Egyptians,

Πεποιθότες λαοῖσι καὶ φρικτοῖς ὅπλοις,

with *Il.* M. 153,

Λαοῖσιν καθύπερθε πεποιθότες, ἠδὲ βίηφιν,

and similar passages.

Nor could the writer have described Moses as striking the Red Sea, in the words

Ἔτυψ᾽ ἐρυθρᾶς νῶτα καὶ ἔσχισεν μέσον

should be compared with Ex. ii. 3, 4, ἔθηκεν αὐτὴν εἰς τὸ ἔλος παρὰ τὸν ποταμόν· καὶ κατεσκόπευεν ἡ ἀδελφὴ αὐτοῦ μακρόθεν, μαθεῖν τί τὸ ἀποβησόμενον αὐτῷ. κατέβη δὲ ἡ θυγάτηρ Φαραὼ λούσασθαι ἐπὶ τὸν ποταμόν, καὶ αἱ ἅβραι αὐτῆς παρεπορεύοντο παρὰ τὸν ποταμόν.

This coincidence in language shews clearly that Ezekiel is versifying the Septuagint; nor is his acquaintance limited to the passage which he is working on, for he shews a general acquaintance with the LXX.: for example, Moses' rod works miracles on the waters of Egypt,

πρῶτον μὲν αἷμα ποτάμιον ῥυήσεται
πηγαί τε πᾶσαι, χ᾽ ὑδάτων συστήματα·

the last expression is taken from the first chapter of Genesis.

[1] He is describing the appearance of a splendid bird which appeared to the Israelites (presumably an omen of Moses himself), twice as large as an eagle, and splendidly coloured; which all the other birds follow as a king.

unless he had been familiar with the Homeric

εὐρέα νῶτα θαλάσσης.

When we turn from poet Ezekiel to poet Theodotus we see the same phenomenon, with the advantage this time that the poem is written in epic metre.

The writer is well acquainted with Homer, from whom he borrows freely, generally disguising his theft by some slight modification in the language. When Simeon and Levi slay Hamor and the Shechemites they do it in right Trojan style:

ὤρουσεν ἐπ' αὐτόν
Πλῆξέ τέ οἱ κεφαλήν, δειρὴν δ' ἕλεν ἐν χερὶ λαιῇ,
Λεῖψε δ' ἔτι σπαίρουσαν, ἐπεὶ πόνος ἄλλος ὀρώρει.
Τόφρα δὲ καὶ Λευὶν μένος ἄσχετος ἔλλαβε χαίτης
Ἁπτόμενον γούνων Συχέμ, ἄσπετα μαργήναντα,
Ἤλασε δὲ κληῖδα μέσην. δῦ δὲ ξίφος ὀξύ
Σπλάγχνα διὰ στέρνων, λίπε δὲ ψυχὴ δέμας εὐθύς.

Here we recognize the Homeric phrases πόνος ἄλλος ἔπειγεν (*Od.* λ. 54), μένος ἄσχετος (*Od.* γ. 19 etc.), τὸν βάλ' ὑπὸ κληῖδα μέσην (*Il.* P. 309); cf. also *Il.* Φ. 116,

Ἀχιλεὺς δὲ ἐρυσσάμενος ξίφος ὀξύ
Τύψε κατὰ κληῖδα παρ' αὐχένα, πᾶν δέ οἱ εἴσω
Δῦ ξίφος ἄμφηκες.

But we also see the artist at work concealing his art by the substitution of feeble alternatives.

So when the writer describes the impiety of the men of Shechem and their lawless state, he contrasts them with the Cyclopes,

οὐ γὰρ ἀάτος
Εἰς αὐτοὺς ὅστις κε μόλῃ καλὸς οὐδὲ μὲν ἐσθλός.
Οὐδὲ δίκας ἐδίκαζον ἀνὰ πόλιν οὐδὲ θέμιστας,

where we recognize the refrain of *Od.* ι. 215,

Ἄγριον, οὔτε δίκας εὖ εἰδότα οὔτε θέμιστας.

Surely, too, we must correct the printed text in the third line of our first extract from ἔτι σπαίρουσαν to ἔτ' ἀσπαίρουσαν which recalls Il. M. 203,

ζωὸν, ἔτ' ἀσπαίροντα.

How easily might this writer have been an actual Centonist!

This case of intimate acquaintance with Homer would be more striking still if Schürer were correct in supposing that the author belonged to the city whose fortunes he describes. Schürer in his *History of the Jewish People*[1] affirms this on the ground that the city is described as a holy city,

Ἡ δ' ἱερὴ Σικίμων καταφαίνεται, ἱερὸν ἄστυ,

from whence we are to infer that the writer is a Samaritan. The only objection would seem to be that the case is parallel to the Homeric descriptions, such as ἄστυ κιχείομεν Ἰλίου ἱρῆς (Il. Φ. 128), which renders the conclusion a little insecure. On the other hand, the writer knew the geographical situation of the city in the valley between Ebal and Gerizim:

Ἐξ αὐτῆς δὲ μάλ' ἄγχι δύ' οὔρεα φαίνετ' ἐρυμνά,
Ποίης τε πλήθοντα καὶ ὕλης· τῶν δὲ μεσηγὺ
Ἀτραπιτὸς τέτμητ', ἀραιή·......

Perhaps, then, we shall at least be safe in regarding the writer as a Palestinian.

That he was also acquainted with the Septuagint will appear from a scrutiny of the proper names in the poem: he calls the city Σίκιμα, and the rulers of it Ἐμὼρ and Συχέμ, which agrees closely with the Greek Bible; we have also Ἀβραάμ, Ἰακώβ, Συμεών, Λευί, and Δείνα, which at all events do not contradict the theory of acquaintance with the LXX.

The third writer to whom we alluded is Philo, the epic poet, who writes the history of Jerusalem. He seems to have been acquainted with the city, for he describes the great aqueduct which, even in his day, brought water from beyond Bethlehem into the sanctuary. The fragments preserved by Eusebius[2] are

---

[1] Theil ii. 750, Eng. Trans. vol. III. p. 228.
[2] *Praep. Evang.* IX. 20, 24, 37.

very rough hexameters, and do not, at first sight, betray any trace of acquaintance with Homer. But a closer study reveals the same feature which we noted in previous cases. Take, for example, the following lines:

Τοῖσιν ἕδος μακαριστὸν ὅλης μέγας ἔκτισεν ἄκτωρ
Ὕψιστος, καὶ πρόσθεν ἀφ᾽ Ἀβραάμοιο καὶ Ἰσάκ,
Ἰακὼβ εὐτέκνοιο τόκος Ἰωσήφ, ὃς ὀνείρων
Θεσπιστὴς, σκηπτοῦχος ἐν Αἰγύπτοιο θρόνοισι,
Δινεύσας λαθραῖα χρόνου πλημμυρίδι μοίρης.

Whatever may be said of the present state of the verses, and certainly they need some correction, the conjunction ἕδος ἔκτισεν is Homeric, for it is the expression used of the founding of Thebes by Amphion and Zethus:

Οἳ πρῶτοι Θήβης ἕδος ἔκτισαν ἑπταπύλοιο

(*Od.* λ. 263),

and the parallel between the verses now shews that we ought to expect the name of the ἕδος, which leads us to correct the unnecessary μέγας into Γέσεμ, from which it may have been derived by transposition of the letters, or we may write Ῥαμεσῆς κτίσεν ἄκτωρ, which would explain why one MS. reads μέσας for μέγας, and would bring the line into very close agreement with the verse in Genesis (xlvii. 11), καὶ κατῴκισεν Ἰωσὴφ τὸν πατέρα αὐτοῦ καὶ τοὺς ἀδελφοὺς αὐτοῦ καὶ ἔδωκεν αὐτοῖς κατάσχεσιν ἐν γῇ Αἰγύπτῳ, ἐν τῇ βελτίστῃ γῇ, ἐν γῇ Ῥαμεσσῇ καθὰ προσέταξε Φαραώ.

The last line of the extract is obscure; I suspect that we have in δινεύσας λαθραῖα an interpretation of the mysterious Zaphnath Paaneah, which has been expanded, for metrical necessity, by the concluding words, producing the line "Eddying the secrets of Time, in the full-tide of destiny." But whether this be the correct explanation or not, enough has been said to shew that there is some ground for believing that Philo, the epic poet, also was acquainted with the Greek Bible, and was a student of Homer, which is, indeed, as we have said, the Greek Bible of an earlier period.

Closely connected with this group of writers we must place the earliest fragments of the Judæan Sibyl, which are, like the poems of Ezekiel and the others, largely Homerized, and undergo exactly similar treatment at the hands of Alexander Polyhistor and the subsequent writers who appropriate his excerpts. It is interesting to notice the retranslation of the Sibylline poetry into prose, and the changes which come over the narrative: the principal passage to which we refer is *Sib.* III. 97—113, to which we append the Homeric parallels from the edition of Rzach:

'Αλλ' οπότ' αν μεγάλοιο θεού τελέωνται απειλαί,
"Ας ποτ' επηπείλησε βροτοις, ότε πύργον έτευξαν,
Χώρη εν 'Ασσυρίη· ομόφωνοι δ' ήσαν άπαντες.
Και βούλοντ' αναβήναι ες ουρανόν αστερόεντα.   *Il.* O. 371
Αυτίκα δ' αθάνατος μεγάλην επέθηκεν ανάγκην   *Il.* Υ. 292
Πνεύμασιν· αυτάρ έπειτ' άνεμοι μέγαν υψόθι   Callim. *Hymn.*
πύργον   in Jov. 30
'Ρίψαν και θνητοίσιν επ' αλλήλους έριν ώρσαν.   *Od.* γ. 161
Τούνεκά τοι Βαβυλώνα βροτοί πόλει ούνομ' έθεντο.   *Il.* Z. 334
Αυτάρ επεί πύργος τ' έπεσεν γλώσσαί τ' ανθρώπων   *Il.* Β. 804
Παντοδαπαίς φωνήσι διέστραφον, αυτίχ' άπασα
Γαία βροτών πληρούτο μεριζομένων βασιλειών.
Και τότε δη δεκάτη γενεή μερόπων ανθρώπων,   *Il.* Α. 250
                                                      Od. ξ. 327
'Εξ ου περ κατακλυσμός επί προτέρους γένετ' άνδρας.
Και βασίλευσε Κρόνος και Τιτάν Ιαπετός τε   *Il.* Θ. 479
Γαίης τέκνα φέριστα και Ουρανού εξεκάλεσσαν
"Ανθρωποι γαίης τε και ουρανού ούνομα θέντες,
Ούνεκά τοι πρώτιστοι έσαν μερόπων ανθρώπων.

There is no doubt about the acquaintance of this writer with the Homeric literature; nor, in spite of the modification introduced into the story, of the destruction of the tower by winds, is there any reason to doubt that he is versifying the Biblical account; the fourth line versifies Gen. xi. 1, the eleventh line Gen. xi. 9, while the mention of the ten generations from the Flood agrees with the genealogy which follows in Gen. xi. 10—32. All of this is very instructive, for we see the attempt already made to furnish Homeric parallels to the Biblical account; the author takes Homer very seriously, and is thus one stage removed from the Centonist proper, who only wants literary parallelism.

Now let us see how this Sibylline translation is taken. First of all there are writers who simply quote it in verse form, either directly as Theophilus, *ad Autolycum* II. 31, or Tertullian, who turns it word for word into Latin, as follows:

Ad Nationes, II. 12, ea (sc. Sibylla) senario versu in hunc sensum de Saturni prosapia et rebus eius exponit. decima, inquit, genitura hominum ex quo cataclysmus prioribus accidit, regnavit Saturnus et Titan et Japetus, Terrae et Coeli fortissimi filii.

Next there is Alexander Polyhistor, who paraphrases the versification back into plain prose as follows:

Σίβυλλα δέ φησιν ὁμοφώνων ὄντων πάντων ἀνθρώπων τινὰς τούτων πύργον ὑπερμεγέθη οἰκοδομῆσαι, ὅπως εἰς τὸν οὐρανὸν ἀναβῶσι· τοῦ δὲ θεοῦ ἀνέμους ἐμφυσήσαντος ἀνατρέψαι αὐτοὺς καὶ ἰδίαν ἑκάστῳ φωνὴν δοῦναι, διὸ δὴ Βαβυλῶνα τὴν πόλιν κληθῆναι· μετὰ δὲ τὸν κατακλυσμὸν Τιτᾶνα καὶ Προμηθέα γενέσθαι. (Euseb. *Chron.* I. 24 e Syncello.)

Polyhistor is borrowed by Josephus in the following manner:

Περὶ δὲ τοῦ πύργου τούτου καὶ τῆς ἀλλοφωνίας τῶν ἀνθρώπων μέμνηται καὶ Σίβυλλα λέγουσα οὕτως· Πάντων ὁμοφώνων ὄντων τῶν ἀνθρώπων πύργον ᾠκοδόμησάν τινες ὑψηλότατον, ὡς ἐπὶ τὸν οὐρανὸν ἀναβησόμενοι δι' αὐτοῦ· οἱ δὲ θεοὶ ἀνέμους ἐπιπέμψαντες ἀνέτρεψαν τὸν πύργον καὶ ἰδίαν ἑκάστῳ φωνὴν ἔδωκαν· καὶ διὰ τοῦτο Βαβυλῶνα συνέβη κληθῆναι τὴν πόλιν. (*Ant. Jud.* I. 4. 3.)

Observe how history is made, and poetry unmade. It would not be easy for us, given the passage from Polyhistor, or Josephus, with the statement that it was a Sibylline oracle, to collect the *disjecta membra poetae*. Traces of the same Sibylline account may be seen in the extracts of Abydenus preserved by Eusebius, and in an extract of Eupolemus preserved by Polyhistor and copied from Polyhistor, by Eusebius. The last passage is as follows:

(Euseb. *Praep. Ev.* IX. 17) Εὐπόλεμος δὲ ἐν τῷ περὶ Ἰουδαίων τῆς Ἀσσυρίας φησί, πόλιν Βαβυλῶνα πρῶτον μὲν κτισθῆναι ὑπὸ τῶν διασωθέντων ἐκ τοῦ κατακλυσμοῦ· εἶναι δὲ αὐτοὺς γίγαντας, οἰκοδομεῖν δὲ τὸν ἱστορούμενον πύργον. Πεσόντος δὲ τούτου διὰ τῆς τοῦ Θεοῦ ἐνεργείας, τοὺς γίγαντας διασπαρῆναι καθ' ὅλην τὴν γῆν. Δεκάτῃ δὲ γενεᾷ φησὶν ἐν πόλει τῆς Βαβυλωνίας Καμαρίνῃ κτέ.

The sequence shews clearly that we have here an abbreviated paraphrase of the Sibylline verses, yet Polyhistor does not seem to have recognized this, nor Eusebius. We see, on every hand, that *the versification (in Homeric and other forms) of the Scripture immediately takes rank as history, even when paraphrased back into prose, and appears as fresh evidence along with the account from which it is derived.* This is true not only of the passage quoted from the Sibyl; it applies to the three earlier writers whom we quoted, all of whom appear as authorities in Clement, Josephus, and Eusebius!

Observe further, that whenever a portion of Scripture or other material has been Homerized, there is a tendency to put it back again into prose by way of paraphrase. We have seen this in the case of the Sibylline verses, which are quoted by writers as Sibylline and yet in prose. Another case of the same kind may be seen in the pages of Hermas, to whom the Church (in the form of the Cumæan Sibyl) reads some fearful prophecies, followed by some sentences, which Hermas records, of a more gentle character, as follows:

Ἰδοὺ ὁ θεὸς τῶν δυνάμεων, ὃς ἀγανῷ δυνάμει καὶ κραταιᾷ καὶ τῇ μεγάλῃ συνέσει αὐτοῦ κτίσας τὸν κόσμον, καὶ τῇ ἐνδόξῳ βουλῇ περιθεὶς τὴν εὐπρέπειαν τῇ κτίσει αὐτοῦ, καὶ τῷ ἰσχυρῷ ῥήματι πήξας τὸν οὐρανὸν καὶ θεμελιώσας τὴν γῆν ἐπὶ ὑδάτων, καὶ τῇ ἰδίᾳ σοφίᾳ καὶ προνοίᾳ κτίσας τὴν ἁγίαν ἐκκλησίαν αὐτοῦ, ἣν καὶ ηὐλόγησεν, ἰδοὺ μεθιστάνει τοὺς οὐρανοὺς καὶ τὰ ὄρη καὶ τοὺς βουνοὺς καὶ τὰς θαλάσσας, καὶ πάντα ὁμαλὰ γίνεται τοῖς ἐκλεκτοῖς αὐτοῦ, ἵνα ἀποδῷ αὐτοῖς τὴν ἐπαγγελίαν ἣν ἐπηγγείλατο μετὰ πολλῆς δόξης καὶ χαρᾶς ἐὰν τηρήσωσιν τὰ νόμιμα τοῦ θεοῦ ἃ παρέλαβον ἐν μεγάλῃ πίστει. (Hermas, *Vis.* I.)

The obvious explanation of this passage, without which the allusions of Hermas to the Sibyl are almost meaningless, is that they are a paraphrase of a set of lost Sibylline verses[1]. We suspect, indeed, that the dread prophecy which Hermas does not quote was an intimation of the impending ruin of Rome, something like what we find in the eighth book of the *Sibylline Oracles*, where the word ῥώμη is made to yield up the number of the years of the life of the city from the foundation to the end; and since this number is 948, the fall of the city was expected by

---

[1] We find the same kind of thing going on in later writers. The verses of Greg. of Nazianzus had a similar fate; if at least we may judge from the MS. Burdett Coutts, II. 7, where the hexameters on the genealogy of the Lord are accompanied by an interlinear paraphrase in red ink.

the initiated in the year 196 A.D. Possibly Hermas may have had something similar in mind.

Parallels to the language of Hermas may readily be found in the existing Sibylline texts; we might, for instance, compare *Sib.* VIII. 235 :

Ὑψώσει δὲ φάραγγας, ὀλεῖ δ' ὑψώματα βουνῶν,
Ὕψος δ' οὐκ ἔτι λοιπὸν ἐν ἀνθρώποισι φανεῖται,

but the actual sequence of Hermas is, I think, not extant. For another case of paraphrased Sibylline verses with a Homeric base we might refer to *Sib.* v. 93—110, which is quoted in Cod. Paris 1043, accompanied by a prose text. The verses are these:—

Ἥξει γὰρ Πέρσης ἐπὶ σὸν νάπος ὥστε χάλαζα,
Καὶ γῆν πᾶσαν ὀλεῖ ἅμα τ' ἀνθρώπους κακοτέχνους
95 Αἵματι καὶ νεκύεσσι......ἱεροῖς παρὰ βωμοῖς   *Il.* Φ. 325 }
   Od. γ. 273}
Βαρβαρόφρων σθεναρὸς πολυαίματος ἄφρονα λεύσσων,
Παμπληθεῖ ψαμαθηδὸν ἐπαιγίζων ἐς ὄλεθρον
Καὶ τότ' ἔσῃ, πόλεων πολυολβος, πολλὰ καμοῦσα.   *Od.* ξ. 65
Κλαύσεται Ἀσὶς ὅλη δώρων χάριν, οἷς ἀπὸ σεῖο
100 Στεψαμένη κεφαλὴν ἐχάρη, πίπτουσ' ἐπὶ γαίης.
Αὐτὸς δ' ὡς Περσῶν ἔλαχεν γαῖαν πολεμίξει
Κτείνας τ' ἄνδρα ἕκαστον ὅλον βίον ἐξαλαπάξαι,   *Il.* H. 424}
   Il. Δ. 40 }
Ὥς τε μένειν μοῖραν τριτάτην δειλοῖσι βροτοῖσι.   *Il.* X. 31}
   Od. δ. 97}
Αὐτὸς δ' ἐκ δυσμῶν ἐσπτήσεται ἅλματι κούφῳ
105 Συμπᾶσαν γαῖαν πολιορκῶν καὶ κατερημῶν.
Ἀλλ' ὅτ' ἂν ὕψος ἔχῃ, κράτερον καὶ τάρβος ἀηδές,
Ἥξει καὶ μακάρων ἐθέλων πόλιν ἐξαλαπάξαι.   *Il.* Δ. 40
Καί κέν τις θεόθεν βασιλεὺς πεμφθεὶς ἐπὶ τοῦτον
Πάντας ὀλεῖ βασιλεῖς μεγάλους καὶ φῶτας ἀρίστους.   *Od.* δ. 530
110 Εἶθ' οὕτως κρίσις ἔσται ὑπ' ἀφθίτου ἀνθρώποισιν.

(*Sib.* v. 93—110, ed. Rzach.)

Of which the paraphrase is as follows:

ἑρμηνεία· ἰδοὺ εἰς αὐτὴν τὸν Πέρσην λέγει ἔρχεσθαι σὺν τῷ ἀντιχρίστῳ, ἕως δυσμῶν μολύνοντα αἵματι καὶ νεκροῖς τὸν ἀέρα καὶ τὰ θυσιαστήρια σὺν πλήθει ψαμμαθίδων ὅμοιον ψάμμου, καὶ λέγει πᾶσαν τὴν γῆν θρηνεῖν τὴν βασιλείαν τῶν Ῥωμαίων καὶ μετὰ τὸ ὑποστρέψαι τὸν Πέρσην ἀπὸ δυσμῶν καὶ ἔρχεσθαι εἰς τὴν ἁγίαν πόλιν σὺν τῷ ἀντιχρίστῳ καὶ μετὰ τὸ πᾶσαν τὴν γῆν ἐρημῶσαι κἀκεῖ καταργεῖσθαι ὑπὸ τῆς παρουσίας τοῦ κυρίου ἡμῶν Ἰησοῦ Χριστοῦ. λέγει γὰρ προνομὴν ποιῆσαι εἰς τὴν ἁγίαν πόλιν τὸν κύριον εἰς κρίσιν δικαίαν ἐν τῇ δευτέρᾳ αὐτοῦ παρουσίᾳ.

Now the first thing we notice in this paraphrase is that the translator begins with an interjected ἰδού, just as we find in the opening of the passage in Hermas. Then we see that the paraphrase is not the work of the modern scribe, but is made from an earlier form of the Greek text than that which is extant either in the Paris extract or elsewhere. For example, the Paris extract reads in l. 94 ἄμ' ἀνδρῶν κακοτέχνῳ, which makes us suspect that the σὺν τῷ ἀντιχρίστῳ of the paraphrase must have had an equivalent in the original verses, different from the edited ἅμα τ' ἀνθρώπους κακοτέχνους. Then the paraphrast certainly found something in his text which answered to ἕως δυσμῶν μολύνοντα, which implies the loss of a verse between 94 and 95. Τὸν ἀέρα of the paraphrast is probably a corruption for τὰ ἱερά; the edited texts shew no sign of this in the verses, reading

παρ' ἐκπάγλοισί τε βωμοῖς,

but the Paris extract has παρεῖ ἐρεῖ sic! καὶ παρὰ βωμοῖς, which suggested to Rzach that the primitive verse contained as its close the words ἱεροῖς παρὰ βωμοῖς. Whatever the original verse may have been, it is clear that the paraphrase is not made immediately from the companion Greek verse[1], and certainly not from the commonly edited text. Enough has been said to shew that there was a tendency to paraphrase and explain Sibylline verses, so that these stand with the previously noted prae-Christian versifications and illustrate vividly the tendencies which we saw at work in them. The question then arises (and it is a very important one), if it be true that the Old Testament records became subject to versification in the manner of Homer and other Greek poets; and if these versifications became the matter for paraphrase; and if the verses and paraphrases alike come to be quoted as independent authorities, distinct from the original texts, are there any similar phenomena in connexion with the text of the New Testament and in the early Patristic literature? Are there any Homerized narratives of the Gospels? Do these find their way in any manner

---

[1] In v. 97 we have first the translation of παμπληθεί into σὺν πλήθει, and then the translator has carried over ψαμαθηδὸν into the paraphrase along with its rendering ὅμοιον ψάμμου, producing the curious result "a host of sand-fishes like sand!"

into prose? And have they any effect upon the faith or the legendary opinions of the early Christian Church? We have already begun to answer these questions in the previous pages. The further working out of the enquiry will be seen in the subsequent chapters.

CHAPTER II.

THE EARLY EDITIONS OF THE CENTONES, AND TRACES OF THEIR USE BY MILTON.

WE now come to the survey of the printed editions of the Centones, and in particular of the *editio princeps* of Aldus, a rare and interesting volume.

Between the years 1501 and 1504 there issued from the Aldine Press four quarto volumes of Greek and Latin Christian Poetry, bound up with some extraneous matter.

The first volume which is dated 1501 contains the works of Prudentius bearing the date, and followed by the hymns of Prosper of Aquitaine, after which comes a collection of Greeks hymns described in the title-page as follows:

Cantica Joannis Damasceni in Theogoniam, Epiphaniam, Pentecosten, in Diem Dominicum Pascae, in Ascensionem, in Transfigurationem, in Annuntiationem.

Cosmae Hierosolymitani. Cantica tredecim.

Cantica Marci episcopi Idrontis in Magnum Sabbatum.

Canticum Theophanis in Annūtionem (*sic*).

These titles are from the first leaf of Prudentius, and they are repeated with some additions at the head of the collection of Greek hymns.

The second volume has the following title-page:

Quae hoc libro continentur.

Sedulii mirabilium diuinorū libri quatuor carmine heroico.

Eiusdem Elegia, in qua finis pentametri est similis principio hexametri.

Eiusdē hymnus de Christo ab incarnatione usque ad ascēsionē.

Juvenci de Euangelica historia libri quatuor.

Aratoris Cardinalis historiae Apostolicae libri duo.

2—2

Probae Falconiae cēto ex Vergilio de nouo et ueteri testamēto.
Homerocentra, hoc est centones ex Homero graece cum interpretatione latina.
Opusculum ad Annūtiationem beatiss. Virginis graece cum latino in medio quaternionum omnium.
Lactantii Firmiani de Resurrectione Elegia.
Eiusdem de passione Domini carmine Heroico.
Cyprianus de ligno crucis uersu Heroico.
Tipherni deprecatoria ad Virginem Elegia.
Oratio ad eandem uersu heroico.
Oratio matutina ad Deum uersu heroico.
Sancti Damasi de laudibus Pauli apostoli uersus hexametri.
Elegia in Hierusalem.
Ode in Natali die Saluatoris.
In die palmarum.
De passione Domini.
Ad Christum ut perdat Turcas.
Epigramma ad beatiss. Virginem.
Vita S. Martini episcopi a Seuero Sulpitio prosa oratione.
De miraculis S. Martini Dialogus, ab eodem.
De trālatione S. Martini, ab eodem.
Vita S. Nicolai a graeco in latinum a Leonardo Justiniano patritio Veneto.

The volume, as printed, does not follow the order of the primitive title; the Centones together with the verses on the Annunciation are removed to the end, and the obvious conclusion is that there was some delay in obtaining the copy of the Greek verses or in doing them into Latin. The major part of the book was in type as early as 1501, for in the middle of the book at the end of the signature *hh* stands the subscription:

Venetiis apud Aldum. MDI mense Januario

(this would in the new style be the beginning of 1502); after the subscription follow the works of Sulpitius Severus etc. Moreover, Aldus' own preface, which is dated

Veñ Mense Iunio M.DII,

states expressly that the volume had been in print for a year ('Christianos poetas, iam annum in thermis nostris excusos').

We cannot very well be in error, therefore, in assigning the

Homeric Centones which close the volume to the year 1502. And that this is the right date will appear also from the privilege for ten years' right of printing, granted to Aldus by the Venetian Government, in which these very volumes are defined. The decree, which was discovered by Baschet in the Venetian Archives, is dated March 23, 1501. It is significant that it does not mention the Homeric Centones as forming part of the book.

We possess two letters of Aldus to John Reuchlin, dated in this very year, in which he speaks of forwarding the Homeric Centones, and explains that the volumes containing Nonnus and Gregory of Nazianzus are not yet ready. Of these letters the first is dated August 18, 1502, and announces the despatch of the first two volumes of the Christian Poets; the second, which speaks of the delay of the other two volumes, to be described presently, is dated December 24, 1502[1]. We assign, then, the first edition of the Centones to the year 1502.

[1] These letters will be found in *Clarorum virorum epistolae ad Johannem Reuchlinum*, Tubingae, 1514; or in Geiger, *Johann Reuchlin's Briefwechsel*, Stuttgart, 1875. The text is as follows:

Aldus Manutius Romanus Joanni Reuchlin Phorcensi s. Amari me abs te plurimum, mi Joannes, iampridem novi, non meo in te ullo officio sed humanitate tua, quare, nisi te benevolentiamque tuam plurimi faciam, sim plane ingratus, sed et facio plurimi et redamo magnopere. Ex libris autem quos petis mitto Julium Pollucem, Stephanum de urbibus, Thucydidem, Etymologicum magnum, Prudentium christianum poetam cum quo et graeca quaedam impressa sunt, Sedulium item cum Juvenco et Aratore, *cum quibus et Homerocentra imprimenda curavi*. Suidas non erat apud me et nuncius tuus dicebat non esse sibi plus pecuniae sed rediturum se brevi Venetias et facturum quod iusseris. Praeterea impressi sunt ex Graecis hi post opera Aristotelis quae a nobis quoque habes: Aristophanes comoediae novem cum commentariis, Epistolae graecae sex et triginta autorum: Dioscorides; Aratus cum Theonis commentariis una cum Julio Firmico; Simplicius in praedicamenta Aristotelis. Ammonius in quinque voces, Gregorii Nazianzeni circiter octo millia carminum, Nonnus carmine heroico in evangelium secundum Joannem, Apollonius poeta cum commentariis. Imprimuntur et quasi absolutae sunt Sophoclis tragoediae septem cum commentariis, item Herodotus. De hebraicis non est impressum quicquam. Quod tu componis placet, perge ut detur studiosis. Impressi sunt praeterea latine literis parvis Virgilius, Horatius, Juvenalis, Persius, Martialis, Lucanus, Catullus, Tibullus, Propertius, Epistolae familiares M. Tulli. Imprimuntur iisdem characteribus Ovidii opera, Statius, Valerius Maximus, si ex his aliquid placuerit, scribe. Interea vale meque ut facis ama. Venetiis. xviii Augusti. Anno MDII.

Aldus Romanus Joanni Reuchlin salutem.

Delectari te plurimum literis et laboribus nostris, Capnion mi, suavissime, quantum ipse delecter, non facile scripserim, tum quia principibus placuisse viris non infima laus est, tum etiam quia laus ista quoniam a te laudato viro proficis-

The preface to the volume dedicates the work to Daniel Clary of Parma, Greek professor in the city of Ragousa. To him Aldus had inscribed the *editio princeps* of Aristophanes in 1498, and to him, two years later, he dedicated the second edition of Homer (1504). The opening sentences are as follows:

Aldus Manutius Ro. Danieli Clario Parmensi in urbe Rhacusa bonas literas publice profitenti S. P. D. Christianos poetas iam annum in thermis nostris excusos tandem mi Clari emittimus, tibique uiro Christianiss. et morum Magistro nuncupamus. qui ne cito, ut ego statueram, et tu optabas, publicarentur, tot mihi impedimento fuerunt, ut ipse mecum saepe sim admiratus, duxerimque κακοδαιμόνων id fieri opera, ne si in locum Gentilium lasciuorumque poetarum, hi nostri Christiani poetae in scholis, ubi teneri puerorum animis instituuntur, succederent, facile in bonos plerique omnes euaderet. Quoniam quo semel est imbuta recens seruabit odorem testa diu. Atque ideo a teneris assuescere multum est......

Vale mi Daniel cum Daniele Restio nostro homine integerr. necnō tam moribus quam literis ornatiss. meque amate ut facitis. Veñ mense Iunio. M.DII.

The preface brings out clearly the object of the edition, the substitution of Christian poetry for pagan in the schools. And this explains also the singular feature of the work, the occupation of the middle of each quaternion of the Centones by a part of another book which has nothing whatever to do with the Centones. The reader who takes up the famous Aldine volume which we are describing will be puzzled to find that after reading a few pages he suddenly passes from Homer into a prose acrostic treatise on the praises of the Virgin. Two pages, Greek and Latin, are occupied in this manner, and then after an intimation that the

citur, facit, ut me esse aliquem putem. Sed deum optimum maximum oro, ut diu alter alterius studio delectari possimus in dies magis, quod non dubito futurum si, quamdiu prodesse hominibus possit vita nostra, uterque vixerimus. Libros omneis quos volebas, cui iussisti dedimus *praeter Nonnum et Gregorium; nondum enim exire in publicum possunt.* Quod vero minoris istic nostros emere libros queas miror. Certum est enim non minoris eo vendi illos Venetiis, quanti constiterunt tibi, immo potius pluris. Sed puto esse causam quoniam mercator iste cum accipiat a societate nostra Venetiis quam plurimos simul libros et minoris quam venduntur singuli ut, quemadmodum aequum est, et ipse lucrari possit aliquid, nec tamen solvat, (damus enim illi ad tempus) gratis eos fortasse habuisse putat. Vale Venetiis 24 Decembris 1502.

rest of the new tract is to be sought in the middle of the next quaternion (Ζείτει sic! τὸ λοιπὸν ἐν τῷ μέσῳ τοῦ ἐφεξῆς τετραδίου), we return to the Centones. The explanation is to be sought, as Renouard[1] points out, in the intention of Aldus to print the opposing Greek and Latin parts of the text so that they could be detached from one another, if need be, and bound up separately. A little consideration will shew that if this is to be accomplished, two successive quires must run as follows:

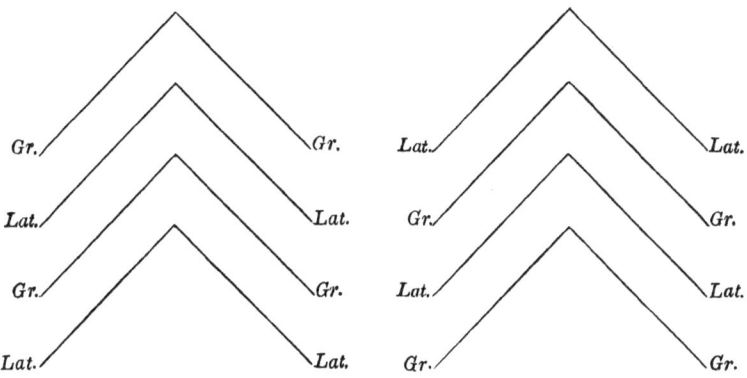

and every sheet can be printed on both sides, except the inside one of each quaternion, which must be left blank.

When Aldus came to the middle of the first quaternion of the Centones, instead of going on with the text, which should have run

περὶ τοῦ εὐαγγελίσμου

with corresponding Latin, he filled up the blank with some unimportant liturgical prose material on the subject of the Annunciation, and continued this from quire to quire according to need.

Such is the explanation of this peculiar feature of Aldus' bilingual texts; they were to be susceptible of division, presumably for the convenience of educators. A similar change of subject in the middle of successive quaternions will be found in the third volume of the Aldine Christian poets, which contains the works of Gregory of Nazianzus. Here the inserted text is the

[1] *Annales de l'Imprimerie*, I. 75.

Gospel of John, set up not from a current text of the Gospel, but from a lectionary beginning, as usual, with the lesson for Easter Day, and ending (in the last duernion *oo*) with John vi. 58 (ὁ ἐκ τοῦ οὐρανοῦ καταβάς) and an intimation that the rest was to be sought in the next quaternion. But no more of the text appeared. Nor is the reason far to seek. For Aldus intimates that he intended the remainder of the lectionary to be employed in the middle of the quires of the Nonnus, which was to be the fourth volume of the series. The Greek of Nonnus was ready as early as 1501, but no Latin was ever accommodated to it[1], and the volume was finally issued without a date, probably about the same time as the Gregory which bears the mark

Venetiis ex Aldi Academia mense Iunio M.DIIII.[2]

[1] Renouard, *Annales*, I. 438.

[2] This is, I believe, the first volume in which the Aldine Anchor and Dolphin appear. The origin of this symbol can be found in the Poliphilus which Aldus printed in 1599. For amongst the beautiful engraved plates which adorn this edition will be found one which contains the famous symbol, described by Poliphilus [Colonna] as 'Una ancora sopra la stangula della quale se rouoluea uno Delphino,' or as it stands in the Old English version, "On the other side was there ingrauen a cyrcle, then an Anchor with a Dolphin winding about the Strangula thereof, which I coniectured should signifie thus

ἀεὶ σπεῦδε βραδέος
Semper festina   tarde."

I suppose that Poliphilus means the circle to be an emblem of eternity ($=ἀεί$), the dolphin of speed ($=σπεῦδε$), and the anchor of resistance to motion ($=βραδέως$). A comparison of the plate in Poliphilus with the Aldine device will make the identification certain, and the text shews that it means 'Festina lente.' But if any doubt remained on the point, a reference to Erasmus' *Adagia* (2. 2. 1) will decide the question. For Erasmus points out that the proverb was a favourite one with Augustus and Titus, and in the case of the latter says:

Iam uero dictum idem Tito Vespasiano placuisse, ex antiquissimis illius nomismatis facile colligitur, quorum unum Aldus Manutius mihi spectandum exhibuit argenteum veteris planeque Romanae sculpturae, quod sibi dono missum aiebat a Petro Bembo patritio Veneto, iuuene cum inter primos erudito, tum omnis literariae antiquitatis diligentissima peruestigatore. Nomismatis character erat huiusmodi: altera ex parte faciem Titi Vespasiani cum inscriptione praefert, ex altera ancoram, cuius medium ceu temonem Delphin obuolutus complectitur. Id autem symboli nihil aliud sibi uelle, quam illud Augusti Caesaris dictum σπεῦδε βραδέως, indicio sunt monimenta literarum hieroglyphicarum......

Scripsit de his rebus Plutarchus in commentario de Osiride et Chaeremon apud Graecos, testimonio Suidae, cuius ex libris excerpta suspicor ea, quae nos nuper conspeximus huius generis monimenta, in quibus etiam haec inerat pictura: Primo loco circulus: deinde ancora, quam mediam, ut dixi, Delphinus obtorto corpore circumplectitur. Circulus ut indicabat interpretamentum adscriptum, quoniam nullo finitur termino, sempiternum innuit tempus. Ancora quoniam nauim

Returning now to the edition of the Homeric Centones contained in the second volume of the series, we have first a preface of Petrus Candidus (Πέτρος Κάνδιδος ὁ μοναχὸς Ἄλδῳ τῷ μανουκίῳ εὖ πράττειν), who affirms that he had transcribed and corrected the text for Aldus, and begs that it may speedily be printed in order that he may present a copy to the Abbot Petrus Delphinus: (καὶ ταῦτα ὡς ἂν Πέτρος ὁ Δελφῖνος, ὁ τῆς ἐρήμου καὶ τάξεως τῆς καμαλδολείας μέγας ἀββᾶς, ταύτης γοῦν τῆς δωρεᾶς, τῆς ἀνδρὸς ἁγιότητι μάλιστα πρεπούσης, ὑπ' ἐμοῦ μεταδοθείη· ἔρρωσο).

Then follow six elegiac lines

Σκιπίωνος καρτερομάχου.
Εἰ τὸ δοκεῖν, μύθοισιν ἐπέτρεπεν αὐτὸν Ὅμηρος,
  Ἀλλ' ἱεροῖς πάντως, ἤθελε ταῦτα πρέπειν.
Θαῦμα γὰρ, εἴτ' ἄλλως γε λελεγμένα, πολλὸν ἀπ' αὐτῶν,
  Τοῖς θείοις ἔργοις ἥρμοσ' ἀρειοτέρως.
Ἀλλὰ δ' ὁμηρείων μάλα γ' ἄξιος οὗτος ἐπαίνων
  Ὅστις ἄρ' εἰς τάδε μιν θεῖα μεθηρμόσατο.

The author of these lines is Scipio Fortiguerra (καρτερόμαχος), one of the most learned of Aldus' Academy. He was born at Pistoia in 1466 and died at Florence in 1515[1]. He was a pupil of Angelo Politiano, and his epigrams appear constantly in Aldus' editions, along with much other serious work. He writes an epigram for the Aldine *Aristotle* of 1495: also ten Greek verses for the *Thesaurus Cornucopiae* of 1496; four Greek lines in praise of Aldus in the *Dictionarium Graecum* of 1497. To him Aldus dedicates the *Juvenal and Persius* of 1501; he writes a Greek preface to the *Homer* of 1504 and in the same year Aldus published his *Oratio de laudibus litterarum Graecarum;* he also prepared for the press the Aldine *Demosthenes*.

remoratur et alligat, sistitque, tarditatem indicat. Delphinus, quod hoc nullum aliud animal celerius, aut impetu perniciore, uelocitatem exprimit: quae si scite connectas, efficient huiusmodi sententiam, ἀεὶ σπεῦδε βραδέως, id est, Semper festina lente......

Itaque dictum hoc σπεῦδε βραδέως, ex ipsis usque priscae philosophiae mysteriis profectum apparet, unde ascitum est a duobus omnium laudatissimis imperatoribus ita ut alteri adagionis esset loco, alteri insignium vice, utriusque moribus ingenioque mire quadrans. Nunc uero in Aldum Manutium Romanum, ceu tertium haeredem, deuenit.

The same explanation will be found in Rabelais, *Garg.* 9. IV. 25.

[1] Didot, *Alde Manuce*, p. 453.

Of his singular modesty and learning Erasmus speaks in a letter dated Basle, March 1524, as follows:

"Quum primum adirem Italiam, iam perierat Philippus Beroaldus Bononiensis cuius memoria tum mire celebris erat et gratiosa, et tamen ille decessit me, ut nunc sum, natu minor. Huius cognatum eodem nomine et cognomine referentem illum vidi Romae: iuvenem moribus candidissimus, stilo et eruditione non inferiorem illo maiore, iudicio multorum, ut et mihi visum est, etiam superiorem. Hunc iuvenem fata e terris eripuerunt. Bononiae primum videre contigit Scipionem Carteromachum, reconditae et absolutae eruditionis hominem, sed usque adeo alienum ab ostentatione, ut, ni provocasses, iurasses esse literarum ignarum. Cum eo post Romae fuit mihi propior familiaritas. Et decessit haud multo maior annis quadraginta duobus."

I think it is extremely likely that Fortiguerra, who assisted Aldus in so many other publications, had also a hand in the production of the Centones.

The Greek text, however, was furnished by a monk Petrus Candidus, who was attached to the subdivision of the Benedictine order known as the Camaldunenses, under the religious headship of Petrus Delphinus.

For Petrus Delphinus we have plenty of biographical material. He was born at Venice in 1444 of noble parentage and at the age of 18 joined the Camaldunensians in the monastery of S. Michael Murianus at Venice. He became abbot in 1479 and a year later he was elected General of the Order. His letters were published, in part by himself in 1524 at Venice (a volume which has become extremely rare), and in part, from a transcript of Mabillon, in the collections of Martène and Durand. Amongst the latter series I see no correspondence between himself and Petrus Candidus. It may, however, be regarded as reasonably certain that the monk in question is one of the famous family of Decembrii who flourished in North Italy in the 15th and 16th centuries. It cannot, however, have been Petrus Candidus Decembrius, the translator of Appian (published at Venice in 1472), and papal secretary under Nicolas V.; for he died in 1477. Probably it is some immediate relation of his, either a son or a nephew.

It appears, therefore, that the Centones must have been set up from an Italian MS., perhaps a Venice MS. We have discussed this interesting copy somewhat at length, but not more so than its antiquity demanded; if we have been diffuse the reader can set it down to a love of Homer or of Aldus. We plead guilty to both.

The remaining editions can be disposed of much more rapidly, being, for the most part, mere reprints of the Aldine text. According to Fabricius, there are two octavo Frankfort editions, printed by Peter Brubach, dated 1541[1] and 1554. These contain the Homerocentra and the Virgiliocentones of Proba Faltonia, with the paraphrase of Nonnus.

Next we have the 12° edition of Henry Stephen of 1578, with the very same contents; and then we come to the Jesuit octavo of Claude Chapelet, published at Paris in 1609, of which we shall have more to say presently. From this point we come to the great Patristic Bibliothecae; the Bibliotheca Patristica of De la Bigne published them in 1624, and they appear in the Paris Bibliotheca of 1644: and in later collections.

We are now going to shew that some one of these editions must have been studied by Milton before he wrote his *Paradise Lost*, and that traces of the early Greek and Latin Christian poets are to be expected in his writings.

We must begin by premising certain facts which are well known to the students of Milton; but a little recapitulation is necessary in order to a clearer understanding of the case.

The *Paradise Lost* was finished in 1665, and appeared for the first time in 1667. It is, however, well known that the ground plan of the work had been laid long before, and that, in particular, some of the finest lines in the book were written many years before the main body of the poem, and when the writer had not even decided finally upon the form which the composition was to take. We know from the explicit statement of Milton's nephew Edward Phillips that the original plan proposed was that of a sacred drama, and that "in the fourth book of the Poem there are six (*lege* ten) verses, which several years before the Poem was begun, were shewn to me, and to some others, as designed for the very beginning of the said

---

[1] I have not seen the second Brubach edition.

Tragedy." The lines in question are the magnificent address of Satan to the Sun

> "O thou! that with surpassing glory crowned
> Look'st from thy sole dominion like the God
> Of this new World: at whose sight all the stars
> Hide their diminished heads" etc...

and this statement of Phillips in the memoir attached to the *Letters of State, written by Mr John Milton*, published in 1694, is corroborated by Aubrey, who in 1680 wrote as follows: "In the Book of Paradise Lost there are about six verses of Satan's exclamation to the Sun which Mr E. Phi. remembers about fifteen or sixteen years before ever his Poem was thought of; which verses were intended for the beginning of a Tragoedie which he had designed, but was diverted from it by other business."

Of this intended Tragedy we have the original drafts in the Common-place Book of Milton preserved in the Library at Trinity College, Cambridge. Concerning this book Masson remarks[1] under the date 1639—1640:

"We have the means of knowing, that there was *one* book, or continuous set of sheets of the same folio-sized paper, of which Milton made particular use about this time......[The scribblings] form part of that volume of Milton's manuscripts which has for a hundred and thirty years been one of the most precious treasures of the Library of Trinity College in Cambridge. An examination of the book, and of seven of its pages in particular, furnishes us with the means of more exact information than was to be hoped for respecting the course of Milton's literary plans and studies, not only after his first removal to St Bride's churchyard, but also, as I believe, during the whole term of his residence there and for some time beyond......

It seems to have been already determined by him that the form should be that of a Tragedy with a Chorus, after the Ancient Greek model, and the hesitation seems to have been mainly as to the subject for such a tragedy. Whether should it be from Scripture, or should it be from British History: and, on either supposition, which out of all that might be found should be selected?"

The Trinity MS. contains a long list of special subjects selected

---

[1] *Life of Milton*, vol. II. p. 103.

by Milton as possible material, under the two heads indicated, the Scriptural subjects being apparently selected after a continuous survey of the pages of the Bible, and the historical subjects from a similar study of English History.

So far all is clear, and the only question that arises is about the date to be assigned to the pages that contain the Biblical and Historical suggested subjects. Masson maintains that these pages were written as early as 1640, and points out that the MSS. shew traces of a change which came over Milton's handwriting after his return from his Italian journey[1].

"In specimens of Milton's autograph before the Italian journey, including the draft of his Lycidas written in November 1637, the small letter *e* is all but invariably shaped in the Greek form (ϵ), but after his return from Italy, and probably in consequence of his stay there, his all but uniform habit was to shape it much as we do now (*e*). This furnishes a useful test of date to be applied to Milton's handwriting in many cases: and as applied to the Jottings it is conclusive that they cannot have been made *earlier* than 1639. The Greek form of the *e* is superseded in them by our present form."

Sotheby, who has given lithographed facsimiles of the Milton Jottings in his *Rambles in the Elucidation of the Autograph of Milton*, does not speak quite so decidedly; according to him[2]:

"Those to whom a comparison in the change of handwriting at different periods is interesting will, on carefully going through the pages of facsimiles from the Trinity College Manuscript, have great difficulty in discovering a single instance of the use of the Greek ϵ in any of the writing before the date of 1639; but to come to any decision as to the date of the Autograph of Milton from that circumstance, would be very fallacious, as in the marginal notes in the copy of *Euripides* belonging to Sir Henry Halford, commenced in 1634, the plain *e* and the Greek ϵ frequently occur in the same word."

Upon the whole, however, the evidence seems to be that somewhere about the year 1640, Milton began to make plans for a sacred Tragedy, and amongst the subjects selected there are several alternative outlines of the *Paradise Lost*, as well as a long list of alternative Scriptural subjects.

---

[1] *Life*, p. 121, note.   [2] *Rambles*, p. 99.

Now let us examine one or two features in these outlines; the third draft of *Paradise Lost*, on p. 35 of the MS., begins as follows:

Paradise Lost.   The Persons.
Moses προλογίζει.
Justice. Mercie (erased). Heavenly Love (erased).
Mercie.
Wisdom. [hymne of ye creation.]
Chorus of angels sing a
  Act. 2.
    etc.

Against the words 'Moses προλογίζει' is written:

'recounting how he assumed his true bodie, that it corrupts not because of his [being] with God in the mount [;] declares the like of Enoch and Eliah, besides the purity of ye place that certaine pure winds, dues[1], and clouds preserved from corruption [;] whence exhorts to the sight of God, tells they cannot se Adam in the state of innocence by reason of thire sin.'

The attention of the reader is invited to the words 'Moses προλογίζει[2].'

Now turn to the drafts of Scriptural subjects on p. 36 of the Trinity MS. The subjects follow in the main the order of the Scriptures, chapters and verses being generally given for reference. But in the left-hand top corner of the page we have several subjects suggested, without references, beginning as follows:

The Deluge. Sodom.
    Dinah vide Euseb. praeparat. Evang. l. 9. c. 22.
the persons
  Dine | Hamor
  Debora rebeccas nurse | Sichem
  Jacob | Counselors 2
  Simeon | Nuncius
  Levi | Chorus.

[1] He was working on some patristic explanation of the preservation of the bodies of Saints by the dew of Paradise. Thus we find in the *Descensus ad Inferos* Isaiah saying: "praedixi vobis exsurgent mortui, et resurgent qui in monumentis sunt, et exsultabunt qui in terris sunt, quoniam ros, qui est a domino, sanitas est illis."

[2] In the first draft of *Paradise Lost* (p. 35 of Common-place Book) the prologue

Now here we have a tragedy planned, with distinct reference to the poem of Theodotus on the destruction of Shechem. And the only question to ask is this: Did Milton in reading the Scriptures through in search of subjects remember that the destruction of Shechem had been already done into an epic poem, and that portions of it were to be found in Eusebius, or had he seen the extracts of Eusebius arranged in order in the pages of some volume of Poetae Graeci Christiani? That he was influenced by Theodotus is certain, but was it the Theodotus latent in Eusebius or the edited Theodotus?

When we recall the 'Moses προλογίζει' of the designed Tragedy of *Paradise Lost,* and observe that Ezekiel's tragedy of the Exodus in the Jesuit volume of 1609 has precisely this feature on its title-page, at the end of the list of persons, we can hardly avoid the conclusion that Milton had been studying the little volume in question or some very similar volume when he made his forecast of possible Sacred Dramas. Nor is there anything *a priori* unlikely in such a supposition, in the case of such a voluminous reader as Milton was; nothing was more in his manner than that he should examine into the previous attempts which had been made at the versification of the Scriptures. A little lower down in the MS. (p. 41) we find suggested for dramatization a New Testament subject as follows:

Christus Patiens. The scene in the Garden, beginning from the coming thither till Judas betrays and the officers lead him away. The rest by message and chorus. His agony may receive noble expression.

The title shews that he knew the famous Euripidean poem, commonly ascribed to Gregory of Nazianzus. There is then nothing improbable in the supposition that Milton had made himself acquainted with the Poetae Christiani of earlier days.

But here we find ourselves in a difficulty; we observe Milton's reference to Eusebius contains the chapter (c. 22). So far as I know this implies a later date than 1628; for in the Stephen edition of the *Praeparatio* (1544) the text is not divided into chapters, while in the Paris text of 1628 the chapters appear.

is given to Michael, but corrected to Moses; so in the second draft. In the fourth draft (on p. 49) the angel Gabriel prologizes, and the work is now called 'Adam unparadised.' It is wonderfully suggestive of the actual work.

Whether there is an edition intervening between these two I do not know, but I think not. This would, at first sight, seem to exclude the volume of 1609[1], as well as the Bibliotheca Patristica of 1624[2], and that of 1644.

I do not see my way to decide more definitely the question as to the edition from which Milton drew. But it is sufficiently clear that he did not neglect the Poetae Christiani. In some form or other these must be included amongst the intellectual treasures of which Hallam speaks so eloquently in his *Introduction to the Literature of Europe*[3] when he says that 'the remembrance of early reading came across his dark and lonely path like the moon emerging from the clouds. Then it was that the Muse was truly his: not only as she poured her creative inspiration into his mind, but as the daughter of Memory, coming with fragments of

---

[1] There is indeed a chapter mark on the Latin side for the extracts from Theodotus (*Euangelicae Praeparat.* lib. 9. c. 4), but this is an older capitulation belonging to a Latin Eusebius. It is, of course, possible that Milton corrected the Latin chapter quoted to the Greek capitulation; he seems to have been fastidious on such points; for I remark in his treatise 'Of reformation touching Church Discipline' such an expression as this 'Eusebius relates in his 3rd book, 35 chap., after the Greek number.'

[2] Its title, as far as the drama of Ezekiel is concerned, is as follows:

ἐκ τῶν κλημεντος.
Ἀλεξανδ. στρωμάτων αʹ
περὶ τῆς ἀναστροφῆς τοῦ Μωϋσεως συνάσεται ἡμῖν καὶ
ὁ Ἐζεκιῆλος ὁ τῶν Ἰουδαικῶν τραγῳδιῶν ποιητὴς ἐν
τῷ ἐπιγραφομένῳ δράματι, Ἐξαγωγή.

ἐκ τῶν Εὐσεβιου εὐαγγελιου
προπαρασκευῆς βιβλ. θ.

περὶ τοῦτον (sic) Μώυσον ἐκτεθῆναι ὑπὸ τῆς μητρὸς εἰς τὸ ἕλος
καὶ ὑπὸ τῆς τοῦ βασιλέως θυγατρὸς ἀναιρεθῆναι καὶ
τραφῆναι ἱστορεῖ καὶ Ἐζεκιῆλος ὁ τῶν τραγῳδιῶν
ποιητης ἄνωθεν ἀναλαβὼν τὴν ἱστορίαν ἀπὸ τῶν σὺν
Ἰακὼβ παραγενομένων εἰς Αἴγυπτον πρὸς Ἰωσήφ

τὰ τοῦ δράματος πρόσωπα

| Μωσῆς | Χοῦς | Ὁ θεὸς ἀπὸ βάτου | Σκόπος |
| Σεπφώρα | Ραγουέλ | Ἀγγελος | λείπει ἄλλα. |

Ἐζεκιηλου του των ιουδαικων.
τραγῳδιῶν (sic) ποιητοῦ Ἐξαγωγή
ⲙⲱⲩⲥⲏⲥ ⲡⲣⲟⲗⲟⲅⲓⲍⲉⲓ

This is set up from the 1609 edition, which itself is a reprint of Morel's *editio princeps* of 1590 (Parisiis. E Typographia Steph. Prenosteau). Here, however, we read λείπει ὁ χόρος for λείπει ἄλλα. The 1609 ed. had simply λείπει.

[3] Vol. IV. c. 5.

ancient melodies; the voice of Euripides and Homer and Tasso—sounds that he had loved in youth and treasured up for the solace of his age.' But the range of Milton's reading was not confined to the classics of literature; he read Jewish poets as well as Greek and Italian. Had these early singers any thought that their music was passing into such a mighty resonator? For we may liken Milton to his own loved organ, where

'from one blast of wind
To many a row of pipes the sound-board breathes.'

CHAPTER III.

The Authorship and Date of the Homeric Centones.

THE Aldine edition of the Centones knows nothing of their authorship, the only allusion to which, in the epigram of Fortiguerra, is limited to the statement that the author was worthy of more than Homeric praise. In the Jesuit edition of 1609, however, we have a short table of contents, containing information to the following effect:

Homerici Centones, quos nonnulli ab Eudocia, Theodosii iunioris Augusti uxore, contextos arbitrantur; at ex Zonara etiam et Cedreno constat Pelagium Patricium Zenonis Imperatoris aetate Homerocentra composuisse, atque in catalogo Heidelbergensis Palatinae num. CCCXXVI. Patricius presbyter quidam poematis Homericis versibus concinnati de Christi incarnatione, vita et morte, auctor asseritur, eodemque libro Eudociae epigramma in illa ὁμηρόκεντρα continetur et num. CCCLXXXIII. Patricii Homerocentra seu Christias ex Iliade et Odissea Homerica: Verum Aldus Manutius nullo expresso nomine auctoris hos Centones cum Latina interpretatione circa an. 1504. Venetiis edidit, et H. Stephanus an. 1578. Graecè tantum.

Immediately before the Centones are prefixed two extracts, one from the Bibliotheca Sancta of Sixtus Senensis, attributing the Centones to Eudocia, and describing the work as made *ad imitatationem Probae Falconiae*; and the other an extract which is as follows:

Ex Zonara, Annalium To. iii in vita Basilii Imperatoris et Cedreno.

Zeno imperator Pelagium Patricium, virum eruditissimum et optimum, per causam Paganismi sustulit; cum re vera timeret ne ab illo redargueretur. Extat historia ab eodem Pelagio scripta versibus, ab Augusto Caesare orsa; Homerocentra etiam composuit, aliaque plurima, laude digna.

We may at once dismiss the statement of Sixtus that the Homeric verses are an imitation of the Virgil Centones of Proba. The antiquity both of the Homer and the Virgil Centones may be seen in the following way: St Jerome in his Preface to the Vulgate addressed to Paulinus, speaks of them in the following contemptuous language:

"Quasi non legerimus Homerocentonas et Vergiliocentonas; ac non sic etiam Maronem sine Christo possimus dicere Christianum quia scripsit

>Iam redit et virgo, redeunt Saturnia regna;
>Iam nova progenies caelo demittitur alto;

et Patrem loquentem ad Filium

>Nate, meae vires, mea magna potentia solus;

et post verba Salvatoris in cruce:

>Talia perstabat memorans, fixusque manebat.

Puerilia sunt haec et circulatorum ludo similia, docere quod ignores; imo (ut cum stomacho loquar) ne hoc quidem scire quod nescias."

If now we refer to the printed text of the verses ascribed to Proba, we shall find in the account of the Baptism

>Tum genitor natum dictis compellat amicis,
>Nate, meae vires, mea magna potentia solus;

and in the account of the Crucifixion

>Post mihi non simili poena commissa luetis.
>Talia perstabat memorans fixusque manebat.

It seems clear that the Latin Centones are older than Jerome, and his reference practically carries the Greek verses also. He is referring to real books. Proba has commonly been represented as junior to Jerome. Her book is older. As to the supposed extracts of Zonaras and Cedrenus given above, they are a brief and incorrect summary of the statements of these writers. What Zonaras actually says is that Eudocia completed the attempt of a certain Patricius at writing Homeric Centones, and Cedrenus identifies this Patricius with a Patricius Pelagius who was put to death by the emperor Zeno[1].

The data are inconsistent; for there can be no hesitation in affirming Eudocia to be the learned wife of Theodosius the second, whose heroic poems and translations Photius mentions (though he does not include the Homerocentra in his list)[2]. But Theodosius II. (A.D. 408—450) is a quarter of a century earlier than Zeno (A.D. 474). Hence we are obliged to correct the tradition, which can hardly be valid unless Eudocia completed the work of some other Patricius, of an earlier date than her own and apparently unknown to fame. Now there is the highest probability in the theory that such a collection as we possess in the Aldine edition came into existence by successive stages of growth. The ambiguity as to authorship appears in several other ways: for example, in the *Inventaire Sommaire des MSS. du Supplément Grec* M. Omont gives an account of a tenth century MS. in the National Library (Cod. 388)[3] which ascribes the Centones to three separate authors: viz.: Patricius Episcopus, Eudocia Augusta, and Cosmas of Jerusalem. The entry is as follows: 'De Homericis Centonibus: Βίβλος Πατρικίου (*f.* 2) Homeri Centones Patricii episcopi [add: optimi philosophi], Eudociae Augustae et Cosmae Hierosolymitanae (*f.* 4).' Here the prefixed Βίβλος on two leaves of the MS. is, no doubt, the epigram from the Greek Anthology, which describes the work of Patricius, and has itself been referred by some to Eudocia. The epigram is so important for the contents of Patricius' Centones that we transcribe it in full, with the corresponding sections of the Edited Centones noted on the margin[3].

Ὑπόθεσις· ἀπολογία εὔφημος Ὁμηροκέντρων.

Βίβλος Πατρικίοιο θεουδέος ἀρητῆρος,
Ὅς μέγα ἔργον ἔρεξεν, ὁμηρείης ἀπὸ βίβλου,
Κυδαλίμων ἐπέων τεύξας ἐρίτιμον ἀοιδήν,
Πρήξιας ἀγγέλλουσαν ἀνικήτοιο θεοῖο.

---

[1] From a recently published Königsberg programme entitled "Eudociae Augustae carminum reliquiae editae ab Arthuro Ludwich," I gather the information that the prologue ascribed to Patricius in the MS. is followed by a second prologue of Eudocia, which I add in a note on next page.
[2] Photius, *Bibliotheca*, Codd. CLXXXIII. and CLXXXIV.
[3] *Anthologia Palatina* (ed. Jacobs, I. 119).

De conceptione et e diuino partu	Ὡς μόλεν ἀνθρώπων ἐς ὁμήγυριν, ὡς λάβε μορφὴν Ἀνδρομέην, καὶ γαστρὸς ἀμεμφέος ἔνδοθι κούρης Κρύπτετο τυτθὸς ἐών, ὃν ἀπείριτος οὐ χάδε κύκλος. Ἠδ' ὡς παρθενικῆς θεοκύμονος ἔσπασε μαζόν, Παρθενίοιο γάλακτος ἀναβλύζοντα ῥέεθρον,
De Herodis infanticidio	Ὡς κτάνεν Ἡρώδης ἀταλάφρονας εἰσέτι παῖδας, Νήπιος, ἀθανάτοιο θεοῦ διζήμενος οἶτον·
De diuino baptismate	Ὣς μιν Ἰωάννης λοῦσεν ποταμοῖο ῥέεθροις.
De uocatione apostolorum	Ὥς τε δυώδεκα φῶτας ἀμύμονας ἔλλαβ' ἑταίρους.
De paralytico etc. De caeco	Ὅσσων τ' ἄρτια πάντα θεὸς τεκτήνατο γυῖα, Νούσους τ' ἐξελάσας στυγερὰς βλεφάρων τ' ἀλαωτύν,
De muliere ınguine fluente	Ἠδ' ὅππως ῥέοντας ἀπέσβεσεν αἵματος ὁλκοὺς Ἁψαμένης ἑανοῖο πολυκλαύτοιο γυναικός.
De filia Iairi et De Lazaro?	Ἠδ' ὅσσους μοίρῃσιν ὑπ' ἀργαλέῃσι δαμέντας Ἤγαγεν ἐς φάος αὖτις ἀπὸ χθονίοιο βερέθρου.
De mysterio	Ὥς τε πάθους ἁγίου μνημήια κάλλιπεν ἄμμιν·
De crucifixione	Ὥς τε βροτῶν ὑπὸ χερσὶ τάθη κρυεροῖς ἐνὶ δεσμοῖς, Αὐτὸς ἑκών· οὐ γάρ τις ἐπιχθονίων πολεμίζοι Ὑψιμέδοντι θεῷ, ὅτε μὴ αὐτός γε κελεύοι·
De descensu ad inferos	Ὡς θάνεν, ὡς Ἀΐδαο σιδήρεα ῥῆξε θύρετρα, Κεῖθεν δὲ ψυχὰς θεοπειθέας οὐρανὸν εἴσω Ἤγαγεν ἀχράντοισιν ὑπ' ἐννεσίῃσι τοκῆος,
e Resurrectione	Ἀνστὰς ἐν τριτάτῃ φαεσιμβρότῳ ἠριγενείῃ, Ἀρχέγονον βλάστημα θεοῦ γενετῆρος ἀνάρχου.

There is hardly a word of this that is not Homeric, and the person who wrote it was indisputably capable of making Homeric Centones. The Paris MS. assigns these verses definitely to Patricius[1]. But the epigram also shews without a doubt that

[1] As follows: to which is attached a prologue by Eudocia.

Τούτους μὲν ἐξέθετο Πατρίκιος ἐπίσκοπος.
ἡ δὲ ἀπολογία Εὐδοκίας Αὐγούστης τῆς Ἀθηναίας τῆς
γυναικὸς Θεοδοσίου Αὐγούστου τοῦ νέου υἱοῦ
Ἀρκαδίου βασιλέως αὕτη.
Ἥδε μὲν ἱστορίη θεοτερπέος ἐστὶν ἀοιδῆς.
Πατρίκιος δ', ὃς τήνδε σοφῶς ἀνεγράψατο βίβλον,
Ἔστι μὲν ἀενάοιο διαμπερὲς ἄξιος αἴνου
Οὕνεκα δὴ πάμπρωτος ἐμήσατο κύδιμον ἔργον.
Ἀλλ' ἔμπης οὐ πάγχυ ἐτήτυμα πάντ' ἀγόρευεν,
Οὐδὲ μὲν ἁρμονίην ἐπέων ἐφύλαξεν ἅπασαν,
Οὐδὲ μόνων ἐπέων ἐμνήσατο κεῖνος ἀείδων,
Ὁππόσα χάλκεον ἦτορ ἀμεμφέος εἶπεν Ὁμήρου.

the Centones of Patricius covered nearly all the ground of the edited verses. The treatment may have been scantier, but it is difficult to believe that the subjects were very different from what we possess in the Aldine text when we have so many of them attested by the epigram. This is an important point, because if Patricius is the first recorded Homerizer of the New Testament we are not on that account to assume that his labour was a mere spicilegium with regard to a subsequent harvest. Nor are we to infer that the shortest text which we find extant in MSS. is necessarily the text of Patricius, unless at all events it contains the subjects with which he is credited in his own epigram. On the other hand it is to be remembered that one peculiar feature of Centonism is that it makes a complete work out of each subject proposed for consideration, so that there is no necessary nexus between one subject selected and the next. Consequently a book

Ἀλλ' ἐγὼ ἡμιτέλεστον ἀγακλεὲς ὡς ἴδον ἔργον,
Πατρικίου σελίδας ἱερὰς μετὰ χεῖρα λαβοῦσα,
Ὅσσα μὲν ἐν βίβλοισεν ἔπη πέλεν οὐ κατὰ κόσμον,
Πάντ' ἄμυδις κείνοιο σοφῆς ἐξείρυσα βίβλου.
Ὅσσα δ' ἐκεῖνος ἔλειπεν, ἐγὼ πάλιν ἐν σελίδεσσι
Γράψα καὶ ἁρμονίην ἱεροῖς ἐπέεσσιν ἔδωκα,
Εἰ δέ τις αἰτιόωτο καὶ ἡμέας ἐς ψόγον ἕλκοι,
Δοιάδες οὕνεκα πολλαὶ ἀρίζηλον κατὰ βίβλον
Εἰσὶν Ὁμηρείων τ' ἐπέων πολλ' οὐ θέμις ἐστίν,
Ἴστω τοῦθ' ὅτι πάντες ὑποδρηστῆρες ἀνάγκης.
Εἰ δέ τις ὑμνοπόλοιο σαόφρονα Τατιανοῖο
Μολπὴν εἰσαΐων σφετέρην τέρψειεν ἀκουήν,
Δοιάδας οὕνεκα κεῖνος Ὁμηρείων ἀπὸ βίβλων
Οὔ ποτε συγχεύας σφετέρῃ ἐνεθήκατο δέλτῳ,
Οὐ ξένον, οὕνεκα κεῖνος Ὁμηρείης ἀπὸ μολπῆς,
Κεῖνος δ' ἐξ ἐπέων σφετέρων ποίησεν ἀοιδὴν
Τρώων τ' Ἀργείων τε κακὴν ἐνέπουσαν ἀϋτήν,
Ὥς τε πόλιν Πριάμοιο διέπραθον υἷες Ἀχαιῶν,
Αὐτὴν Τροίαν ἔχουσαν, ἐν ἀργαλέῳ τε κυδοιμῷ
Μαρναμένους αὐτούς τε θεούς, αὐτούς τε καὶ ἄνδρας,
Οὕς ποτε χαλκεόφωνος ἀνὴρ αὔτησεν Ὅμηρος.
Πατρίκιος δὲ ὃς τήνδε σοφὴν ἀνεγράψατο δέλτον,
Ἀντὶ μὲν Ἀργείων στρατιῆς γένος εἶπεν Ἑβραίων,
Ἀντὶ δὲ δαιμονίης τε καὶ ἀντιθέοιο φάλαγγος
Ἀθανάτους ἤεισε καὶ υἱέα καὶ γενετῆρα.
Ἀλλ' ἔμπης ξυνὸς μὲν ἔφυ πόνος ἀμφοτέροισι
Πατρικίῳ κἀμοί, καὶ θηλυτέρῃ περ ἐούσῃ·
Κεῖνος δ' ἤρατο μοῦνος ἐν ἀνθρώποις μέγα κῦδος,
Ὃς πάμπρωτος ἐπήξατο κλεινὸν ἕδος γε δόμοιο
Καλὴν ἐξανάγων φήμην βροτέοιο γενέθλης.

of Centones readily grows: one has only to propose a fresh list of subjects and versify them; and the new composition can be at once attached to the old, without shewing much evidence of junction where the separate parts are brought together. We must not, therefore, assume that Patricius had those sections which we find in the Aldine text, but are not alluded to in the epigram; such, for instance, as deal with the Fall of Man and the resulting Divine economy. Questions of this kind must be reserved for a closer enquiry, and particularly for an enquiry based upon the written traditions of the text[1]. Fortunately we are not limited in our investigation to the discussion of the MSS., for we shall shew presently in a conclusive manner reasons for believing in the existence of a body of Homeric Centones long before the time of Eudocia. Meanwhile it is sufficient to remember that we have already three claimants for the authorship—Patricius, Eudocia and Cosmas; of whom there is some reason to suspect Patricius to be the first, but beyond this we have as yet no light with regard to the questions of date or authorship[2]. If the reference to Cosmas be genuine, the work must have reached its final form in the eighth century. But it is well to remember that the upper limit of the enquiry as to date may be anywhere. The further back we go, the greater is the acquaintance with Homer. Centonism was rife, certainly, in the second century, both in Greek and in Latin. The latter is proved by the testimony of Tertullian[3] as to the transfer of Medea into Virgilian verse; the former, by the interesting specimen quoted by Irenaeus of the descent of Herakles into Hades to fetch the dog Cerberus[4]. If à priori probability counts for anything in an enquiry of this kind, it must be allowed that it is in favour of an early Centonization of portions, at least, of the Biblical narrative. The enquiry is an open one, let us see whither it will lead us.

[1] The principal MSS. to be examined, besides Cod. Paris Suppl. 388 described above, are

    Cod. Reg. 2867 (chart. manu. Angeli Vergecii), which ascribes the verses to Eudocia Augusta. Cod. Reg. 3047 and Cod. Reg. 2755, which refers them to Patricius, and perhaps Cod. Reg. 2891 (cent. xvi.) and 2977.

[2] Eudocia has an obscure reference to Tatian. Which Tatian?

[3] *De Praescript. Haeret.* 39. He also alludes in the same passage to the Homeric Centonists.

[4] Irenaeus, I. ix. 4.

Before we turn to the demonstration of the antiquity of the ground-form which underlies the Homeric Centones, it will be convenient to make a few remarks on the constitution of a Cento.

First of all, a subject is proposed to the pseudo-poet, which he expands and dilates upon in Homeric language. This is the reason for the division of the Edited Centones into a series of chapters. They are not really chapters, but set subjects; and it is even probable that some of the titles have disappeared from the published text, so as to confuse the separate poems.

Then, in considering the Cento as a work of art, it is evident that it would cease to be interesting if many consecutive verses of Homer were quoted ; and it is, therefore, not usual to quote more than two or three adjacent verses. Where this is not adhered to, the Centonist loses his reward of praise; for the credit of the work, and the charm, where it has a charm, is in the junction of disconnected verses, and the adaptation of old sentences to new meanings. Occasionally we shall find our Biblical Homeric Centones to fall under condemnation on this head.

There is an ingenious Cento in the Greek Anthology[1] which will furnish a good instance of how the work ought to be done: the subject proposed is "The man that first heard an Echo," and the verses are as follows:

Ὁ πρῶτος Ἠχοῦς ἀκούσας.

Il. B. 110	Ὦ φίλοι, ἥρωες Δαναοί, θεράποντες Ἄρηος,
Od. δ. 140	Ψεύσομαι ἦ ἔτυμον ἐρέω; κέλεται δέ με θυμός·
Od. ε. 238	Ἀγροῦ ἐπ' ἐσχατιῆς ὅθι δένδρεα μακρὰ πεφύκει,
Od. μ. 150 Od. ε. 58	} Ναίει ἐϋπλόκαμος δεινὴ θεὸς αὐδήεσσα,
Od. κ. 228 Od. μ. 249	} Ἡ θεὸς ἠὲ γυνή· τοὶ δὲ φθέγγοντο καλεῦντες.
Od. ι. 497	Εἰ δὲ φθεγξαμένου του ἦ αὐδήσαντος ἀκούσῃ,
Od. μ. 453	Αὖτις ἀριζήλως εἰρημένα μυθολογεύει.
Il. K. 432	Ἀλλὰ τίη τοι ταῦτα διεξερέεσθε ἕκαστα ;
Od. τ. 478	Τὴν δ' οὔτ' ἀθρῆσαι δύναμ' ἀντίον, οὔτε νοῆσαι.
Il. Υ. 250	Ὁπποῖόν κ' εἴπῃσθα ἔπος, τοῖόν κ' ἐπακούσαις.

The references will enable the reader to see how closely Homer has been followed ; many verses are quite unaltered, and others very slightly : in the third verse, for example, ἀγροῦ has been

[1] Ed. Jacobs, II. 134.

substituted for νήσου[1]. No consecutive verses of Homer occur. Irenaeus' verses on the descent of Herakles follow Homer still more closely, but here the subject was an easier one. We have, however, consecutive verses used, a fact which the writer tries to disguise. The lines are as follows:

Od. κ. 76   Ὡς εἰπὼν ἀνέπεμπε δόμων βαρέα στενάχοντα
Od. φ. 26   Φῶθ' Ἡρακλῆα, μεγάλων ἐπιίστορα ἔργων
Il. T. 123 Εὐρυσθεύς, Σθενέλοιο πάϊς Περσηϊάδαο,
Il. Θ. 368 Ἐξ Ἐρέβευς ἄξοντα κύνα στυγεροῦ Ἀΐδαο.
Od. ζ. 130 Βῆ δ' ἴμεν ὥστε λέων ὀρεσίτροφος ἀλκὶ πεποιθώς,
Il. Ω. 327 Καρπαλίμως ἀνὰ ἄστυ· φίλοι δ' ἅμα πάντες ἕποντο,
Od. λ. 38   Νύμφαι τ' ἠΐθεοί τε πολύτλητοί τε γέροντες,
Il. Ω. 328 Οἴκτρ' ὀλοφυρόμενοι, ὡσεὶ θανατόνδε κίοντα.
Od. λ. 625 Ἑρμείας δ' ἀπέπεμπεν, ἰδὲ γλαυκῶπις Ἀθήνη·
Il. B. 409 Ἤιδεε γὰρ κατὰ θυμὸν ἀδελφεόν, ὡς ἐπονεῖτο.

It would have been natural to quote directly from Il. Θ. 367 as well as 368

Εὖτέ μιν εἰς Ἀΐδαο πυλάρταο προύπεμψεν,

but this was too obvious a verse, and the composer disdained to employ it.

We notice that in each of these cases, the writer contented himself with making a new poem of ten verses. Perhaps this was the conventional limit of the professional Centonist.

But it is in the adaptation of Homer to a non-Homeric subject that the skill of the composer is most apparent. It was easy to write of Herakles and Cerberus, because they were Homeric characters; but when one has to illustrate non-Hellenic scenes, and Semitic surroundings, then comes the test of the artist, and if any praise be due to ingenuity, the composers of the Biblical Centones bear the palm away from all competitors. For example, the lame man whom Christ heals is introduced in the words

Il. P. 465 Ὀψὲ δὲ δή μιν ἑταῖρος ἀνὴρ ἴδεν ὀφθαλμοῖσι,
Il. Σ. 411 Χωλεύων, ὑπὸ δὲ κνῆμαι ῥώοντο ἀραιαί.

It is the limping Hephaestus in disguise!

The woman of Samaria, going into the city to inform the

---

[1] The Epigram is discussed and praised by Henry Stephen in his *Parodiae Morales*.

men of the place concerning the Prophet with whom she has conversed, begins her speech as follows:

Od. θ. 11 Δεῦτ' ἄγε Σικίμων ἡγήτορες ἠδὲ μέδοντες.

It is Athene, whom Homer introduced disguised as a herald, announcing to the Phaecians the arrival of Odysseus, who now, by the substitution of the single word Σικίμων for Φαιήκων, appears in the Oriental garb of the Samaritan woman[1]!

When Thomas makes enquiry as to the reality of the Lord's resurrection, and is shewn the marks of the wounds

Od. τ. 391 Οὐλὴν δ' ἀμφράσαντο, καὶ ἀμφαδὰ ἔργα γένοντο.

It is an adaptation of the boar-mark on Odysseus' thigh, by which the old nurse recognizes him!

The five thousand who eat bread by miracle are described, with a slight liberty taken in the computation by the words

Od. γ. 7 Ἐννέα δ' ἕδραι ἔσαν, πεντηκόσιοι δ' ἐν ἑκάστῃ
[Εἴατο καὶ προύχοντο ἑκάστοθι ἐννέα ταύρους].

The line describes the banquet on the shore of Pylos, when Telemachus comes there in search of his father! And so on, in a variety of other borrowed lines, which were made to reflect the subject which the Centonist was engaged upon. Sometimes this reflection was natural enough; there was no difficulty, for example, in making Eumaeus the swineherd of the Galilean Lake, or in depicting a suitable banquet for the marriage at Cana, though it certainly is a little audacious on the part of the writer to tell us that, in the latter case, the board was decked with swine's flesh:

Il. Ψ. 32 Πολλοὶ δ' ἀργιόδοντες ὕες, θαλέθοντες ἀλοιφῇ,
Εὐόμενοι τανύοντο διὰ φλογὸς Ἡφαίστοιο.

How ingenious is the translation of the sentence in the Gospel, where our Lord commanded that something to eat should be given to the revived maiden:

Od. ζ. 209 καί τε δοτ', ἀμφίπολοι, κούρῃ βρῶσίν τε πόσιν τε.

It is the command of Nausicaa to her maidens to entertain Odysseus, with the single change of κούρῃ for ξείνῳ.

But we shall see plenty of cases of the power of the writer to Homerize whatever subject he laid his hands on. The Centones, though they naturally shew some chasms between the verses, are a marvel of ingenuity, such as, probably, could not be duplicated in the whole range of ancient and modern literature.

[1] Reading Συχὲμ for Συχὰρ as in the Lewis Codex.

CHAPTER IV.

ON THE LITERARY PARALLELISM BETWEEN THE HOMERIC CENTONES AND THE ACTS OF PILATE.

WE now turn aside to examine a famous apocryphal document which has exercised a great influence upon art, literature and theology, the so-called *Acta Pilati*[1]. The work in the forms in which it has come down to us is, in all probability, a product of the fourth century; but the recensions of it are in barbarous Greek, and differ *inter se*; nor has any attempt as yet been successful to reconstruct the earlier form of the Pilate legends which underlies the extant texts and versions.

We may confine ourselves, to begin with, to the text as edited by Tischendorf, who much enriched the critical apparatus for the study of the Acta, and printed a critical text of the different recensions which he detected amongst his MSS. To be more exact, we should say that Tischendorf's text comprises a division of the subject into two parts, which he names respectively the *Gesta Pilati* and the *Descensus ad Inferos*; of the first of these Tischendorf prints two Greek recensions (A and B), and a Latin text; and of the latter he prints two Latin texts (A and B) and a Greek text. I may say at once that there is nothing final about the editing of these texts, and that a fresh examination of the whole subject is much needed. But we need not concern ourselves immediately with the critical difficulties that beset the Editor of the Acta, and which are far greater than a superficial student would imagine. We shall refer to the Tischendorf text, as found in his *Evangelia Apocrypha* (ed. ii), as the standard.

---

[1] Known in the West as the Gospel of Nicodemus. When Erasmus and Colet visited Canterbury Cathedral, they saw a copy of this Gospel chained to one of the pillars for public reading.

The first part of the book is concerned with the account of the apprehension and trial of Jesus before Pilate, and his subsequent crucifixion. When the trial is under way, Nicodemus comes forward to speak in our Lord's behalf, and he is followed by a number of persons who have been the subjects of our Lord's miraculous healing, and in almost every instance they are introduced by the same formula. The procession begins by a paralytic who has been healed, who is seen by an examination of the story which he tells to be the paralytic of thirty-eight years at the pool of Bethesda, compounded with the man sick of the palsy who was carried on his bed and laid down before Jesus. The account opens as follows:

εἷς δὲ τῶν Ἰουδαίων παραπηδήσας ἠξίου τὸν ἡγεμόνα λόγον εἰπεῖν.

The next case is that of a blind man, who is introduced as follows:

καὶ ἄλλος Ἰουδαῖος παραπηδήσας λέγει.

He is followed by a cripple, described similarly,

καὶ ἄλλος Ἰουδαῖος παραπηδήσας εἶπεν.

The next case is that of a leper, who is more briefly introduced by the words,

καὶ ἄλλος εἶπεν.

Now the key-word to the structure of the story lies in this repeated formula and its peculiar παραπηδήσας. It only occurs in recension A, but there is no doubt about its accuracy here, however much we might at first sight wish to correct it to προπηδάω or some more natural word; for in c. xii. the text refers again to the procession of witnesses and speaks of them as τὸν Νικόδημον καὶ ἄλλους ἑτέρους πολλούς, οἵτινες παραπηδήσαντες κτέ. Many of the MSS. of the recension have made attempts to explain the peculiar word, as for example, by the addition of εἰς τὸ μέσον. It does not, however, need any correction; it is a proper word to describe the coming forward of a witness, as may be seen by a reference to Sextus Empiricus[1].

In recension B the prologues to the stories told by the chain of witnesses have been entirely changed, and we have instead of the previous forms such sentences as

[1] *Adv. mathematicos*, p. 556. 31. I owe the reference to Prof. Robinson.

Ταῦτα εἰπόντος τοῦ Νικοδήμου ἕτερος ἐγερθεὶς
Ἑβραῖος λέγει.
Ἕτερος πάλιν σταθεὶς μέσον εἶπεν.
Ἕτερος εἶπε.
Ἄλλος εἶπεν.

The relative simplicity of these sentences suggests that they are a later development of the story, after a process of editing and perhaps of re-translation. The characteristic παραπηδήσας has disappeared, being replaced by ἐγερθείς, σταθεὶς εἰς τὸ μέσον, or altogether omitted.

When we examine the extant versions of the Acta, we find a similar disappearance in the Coptic, where the prologues are now

Alius porro ex Judaeis accessit ad Pilatum dicens:
Item alius Judaeus aiebat:
Alius etiam ad Pilatum accedens dixit:

in which παραπηδήσας has been equated to the Coptic equivalent of *accessit ad Pilatum*.

The Latin version, however, has preserved something of the original trait, and gives us

Ex Judaeis quidam alius autem exsiliens rogat:
Et alius quidam Judaeus exsiliens dixit:
Et alius Judaeus exsiliens dixit:
Et alius dixit:

where the MSS. of the version will, however, be found occasionally correcting *exsiliens* into *prosiliens* or *exiens*: or substituting such paraphrases as *rogavit festinanter*.

Now let us turn to the account of our Lord's miracles in the Homeric Centones. A number of sections are devoted to the various miracles, which are edited in the following order:

περὶ τοῦ παραλύτου.
περὶ τοῦ ἐν τῇ στοᾷ Σολομῶντος ἑτέρου παραλύτου.
περὶ τῆς θυγατρὸς τοῦ ἑκατοντάρχου.
περὶ τοῦ χωλοῦ τοῦ καὶ ξηρὰν ἔχοντος χεῖρα.
περὶ τοῦ τυφλοῦ.
περὶ τοῦ δαιμονῶντος.

Now, without stopping to investigate which particular miracle or combination of miracles is intended in each case (for the writer of the Centones compounds his miracles freely), let us examine the opening sentences of the separate accounts; and we shall find in them the traces of a common introductory verse, which binds the series of subjects together. The story of the paralytic, after a conventional allusion to the Rosy-fingered Dawn, proceeds with

Od. σ. 1 Ἦλθε δ' ἐπὶ πτωχὸς πανδήμιος, ὃς κατὰ ἄστυ
Κεῖτ' ὀλιγηπελέων.

The story of the blind man opens with the lines

Ἄλλος δ' αὖθις πτωχὸς ἀνὴρ ἀλαλήμενος ἐλθὼν
Ἑστήκει, μέγα πένθος ἐνὶ στήθεσσιν ἀέξων.

The story of the demoniac opens with

Ἀλλ' ἄλλος τις πτωχὸς ἀνὴρ ἀλαλήμενος ἐλθὼν
Δεσμῷ ἐν ἀργαλέῳ δέδετο κρατέρ' ἄλγεα πάσχων.

There is no mistaking the significance of these introductory verses; the writer planned a procession of poor men, and the typical verse for introducing them is the Homeric line

Ἀλλ' ἄλλος τις πτωχὸς ἀνὴρ ἀλαλήμενος ἐλθών. *Od. φ.* 327.

Now, when we compare the sequence of the miracles in the Centones and their typical formula of introduction with the procession of witnesses in the Acta who have been healed by Christ, and note the formula with which their testimony is introduced, we shall see that there is some reason to suspect a connexion between the two compositions. The obvious suggestion is that the two formulae

Καὶ ἄλλος Ἰουδαῖος παραπηδήσας

and Ἄλλος αὖθις πτωχὸς ἀνὴρ ἀλαλήμενος ἐλθών

are equivalent: and this may very easily be the case if ἀλαλήμενος had been read or understood as ἁλλόμενος. The sentence in the Acta would be thus a prose paraphrase of a Homeric line; and the different recensions of the Acta would arise from different treatment of the original verse, or from subsequent corrections or translations of the first prose paraphrase[1].

But if our suggestion be a correct one for the explanation of the phenomena, we clearly cannot limit ourselves to the study of a single line; we must examine for further coincidences of treat-

[1] For the existence of the primitive πτωχὸς we shall find suspicious evidence presently, when we come to examine a parallel formula in the *Descensus ad Inferos* (ἦλθεν ἕτερος ταπεινὸς ἄνθρωπος).

ment by the two documents, and we must demonstrate more thoroughly the existence of Homeric influence on the Acta. This we shall be able abundantly to do. For example, we may shew at once that there is a parallelism between the two documents in the matter of the miracles which they discuss. Let us compare the following sequences:

Acta Pilati.	Edited Centones.	Centones from the epigram on Patricius.
1. The paralytic of 38 years who is brought on his bed to Jesus.	1. A paralytic.	1. De paralytico etc.
2. The blind man who cried 'Have mercy on me, Son of David.'	2. Another paralytic in Solomon's Porch.	2. De caeco etc.
3. The deformed man.	3. The daughter of the Centurion (sic!).	
4. The leper.	4. The lame man with the withered hand.	3. De muliere sanguine fluente.
5. The woman named Bernice who had the twelve years' flux.	5. The blind man.	
6. A multitude of men and women who affirm the Lord to be a prophet with power over demons,	6. The demoniac.	4? De filia Jairi et de Lazaro.
	7. Mulier sanguine fluens.	
	8. The Samaritan woman.	
7. and others who testify to the raising of Lazarus.	9. The seven loaves.	
	10. The raising of Lazarus.	

A study of the successive subjects shews that they are connected one with the other. Each series begins with the paralytics and ends with the raising of Lazarus. It is true that there are two separate treatments of the subject of the paralytics in the Edited Centones, but there are two paralytic stories rolled into one in the *Acta Pilati*. Each has the paralytic of John v.: the Acta betray him by the reference to the 38 years; the Centones by the allusion of the poet to the sick man as lying τρητοῖς ἐν λεχέεσσι ὑπ' αἰθούσῃ ἐριδούπῳ, an expression which probably arose out of the five porches in the Gospel[1]. Between the two extremes of the lists there is some variation. But it is noticeable that as far as we are able to trace the order of Patricius it agrees with the order in the Acta, and only differs from that of the Edited Centones in that the case of the daughter of Jairus, which we have supposed included in the allusion to Christ's resurrection miracles, appears in the printed texts as a separate

---

[1] The expression τρητοῖς ἐν λεχέεσσι would seem to exclude the identification with the lame man in *Solomon's Porch*.

subject at an earlier point in the lists. But the resemblance between the Centones and the Acta is too decided to be the result of accident[1].

We may also, by the examination of the text of the Acta in the neighbourhood of the matter previously quoted, satisfy ourselves that there is more Homer underneath. The very next sentence in the account of Nicodemus and the procession of witnesses is a typical one. The entrance of Nicodemus to the court is followed by a speech ἀξιῶ, εὐσεβῆ, κέλευσόν μοι εἰπεῖν ὀλίγους λόγους. In the second recension it runs thus; δέομαί σου τῆς μεγαλειότητός σου ἐᾶσαί με εἰπεῖν πρός σε ὀλίγα τινὰ ῥήματα: and something similar appears in the introduction of the first witness, where the recension (A) records ἠξίου τὸν ἡγεμόνα λόγον εἰπεῖν, and recension (B) δέομαί σου, κύριέ μου Πιλᾶτε, ἄκουσον κἀμοῦ, with the significant variant κέλευσόν με, ἡγεμών, ἕνα λόγον εἰπεῖν, in which we recognize the features of the speech of Nicodemus in recension A. How did all this confusion come about, and what made the writer think of addressing Pilate by the title of εὐσεβής, which would have been too much either for conventional politeness or Christian partiality for the governor? The probable solution is that we have here a variety of workings in prose of a line not very dissimilar from the Homeric verse

(Il. A. 74) Ὦ Ἀχιλεῦ, κέλεαί με, διΐφιλε, μυθήσασθαι,

where we catch the original of κέλευσον, and also see the hard word from which the εὐσεβής arose[2]. What follows in the Acta would then be, naturally enough, an adaptation of the answer of Achilles to Calchas' request

θαρσήσας μάλα εἰπὲ τὸ θεοπρόπιον ὅπερ οἶσθα.

---

[1] There is nothing in the Acta as far as I know to answer to the Samaritan woman; nor any mention of the miracle of the loaves; but it is worthy of notice that one MS. of the Acta has substituted the following sentence for the allusion to the raising of Lazarus:

ἐκ πέντε ἄρτων χιλιάδας ἔθρεψε πέντε,
καὶ ἐν ἑπτὰ ἄρτοις χιλιάδας τέσσαρας καὶ
οἱ δαίμονες αὐτὸν φοβοῦνται.

But this is perhaps, not to be pressed as a coincidence with the Centones.

[2] Here Psellus has in his paraphrase

ὦ τῷ Διὶ προσφιλέστατε Ἀχιλλεῦ, κελεύεις με ἐξειπεῖν καὶ φράσαι.

What we actually find in the *Acta* is in rec. A

$$εἴ τι θέλεις εἰπεῖν, εἰπέ,$$

and in rec. B $εἰπὲ ὅ τι βούλῃ,$

either of which might be a summary of the Homeric line.

It is interesting also to note that it is in the conception of a Homeric base that we find the solution to many of the perplexing variants in the MSS. of the *Acta Pilati*. Here is one striking specimen from the story of the Paralytic. The Acta in recension A tell us that the paralytic's account of himself was as follows:

$$καί τινες νεανίσκοι κατελεήσαντές με ἐβάστασαν$$
$$με μετὰ τῆς κλίνης καὶ ἀπήγαγόν με πρὸς αὐτόν.$$

One of the best MSS. reads $πιστότατοι$ for $νεανίσκοι$. No paleography will explain the variant, but a reference to the story as told in the Centones will shew that both words should stand in the text, and that $πιστότατοι νεανίσκοι$ is the prose paraphrase of the Homeric $ἐρίηρες ἑταῖροι$, the verses borrowed being

$$τὸν μὲν ἔπειθ' ὑποδύντε δύω ἐρίηρες ἑταῖροι^1$$
$$αὐτοῦ κεν προπάροιθε ποδῶν βάλον ἐν κονίῃσι^2.$$

Now if the previous suggestions and arguments are correct, it means that there is an earlier Homeric Gospel somewhere behind the Centones and behind the *Acta*. A common document there must be somewhere; and no conceivable skill could have made the Centones out of a consecutive prose Gospel which has disappeared, in such a way as to preserve the sequences of that Gospel. Even in dealing with the actual Gospel, the subject matter has to be treated very freely, and in fact the Gospel is rather accommodated to Homer, than Homer to the Gospel: it is true that such verses are selected and strung together, as will illustrate some Gospel event, but even the man who had Homer most at his fingers' ends could not always find lines of Homer that would move *pari passu* with the story. Consequently there can be nothing between the Centones and the Gospel which they disguise, except some earlier

---

[1] Psellus renders *Il.* Γ. 47

$$τὴν θάλασσαν ἐπιπλεύσας καὶ ἑταίρους εὐαρμόστους συναγαγών,$$

which does not help us much.

[2] Another remarkable variant is found in the MSS. of rec. A in c. v. We have $ἀξιῶ, εὐσεβή, κέλευσόν μοι εἰπεῖν καθαροὺς λόγους$. This points to a primitive variation of the text of the Homeric parallel to $ἐναίσιμα μυθήσασθαι$ (cf. *Od.* β. 159).

form of the Centones themselves. A prose ground-text is not to be thought of.

The same conclusion is arrived at by a study of the *Acta*, which suggest a metrical basis of their composition. We say then, tentatively, and with the intention of making a more complete demonstration in a subsequent chapter, that a common metrical Gospel underlies the different recensions of the *Acta Pilati* and the extant Centones. It was probably a Greek metrical document or at all events a Homerized story; it may have passed through any number of translations or paraphrases, but the starting point would seem to be a text which reproduced Homer directly.

We shall now shew that the whole of the structure of the Acts of Pilate is Homeric; and that actual fragments of Homer may still be traced in the extant recensions of these Acts.

CHAPTER V.

HOMERIC STRUCTURE OF THE ACTS OF PILATE.

A VERY slight examination of the extant tradition of the *Acta Pilati* will suffice to shew that the book divides into two parts, of which the first is occupied with the trial and condemnation of our Lord, and the second with the history of His descent to the underworld. Accordingly we find that in the Greek text of Tischendorf the first sixteen chapters of the *Acta Pilati* are given by themselves in a double recension, while the last eleven chapters are also edited separately in a single recension. In the Latin text on the other hand we have the first sixteen chapters in a single recension and the last part of the book in a double recension.

The titles attached by Tischendorf are as follows:

i. Greek. Ὑπομνήματα τοῦ κυρίου ἡμῶν Ἰησοῦ Χριστοῦ πραχθέντα ἐπὶ Ποντίου Πιλάτου,

with the current editorial heading *Acta Pilati*, A, and

Διήγησις περὶ τοῦ πάθους τοῦ κυρίου ἡμῶν Ἰησοῦ Χριστοῦ καὶ τῆς ἁγίας αὐτοῦ ἀναστάσεως.

And these two separate recensions are followed by the editorial title for the remaining chapters:

Evangelium Nicodemi, Pars ii,
sive
Descensus Christi ad inferos,

with current heading *Acta Pilati*, Pars ii.

ii. Latin. The Latin Acts are headed by Tischendorf (from Gregory of Tours) *Gesta Pilati*; while the concluding chapters are described as

>Evangelii Nicodemi pars altera,
>sive
>Descensus Christi ad Inferos
>Latine A et B,

with the same title in the head-lines.

Now, without stopping to discuss the form which these titles take in the manuscripts, we can see that the composition must fall into two parts, or how could we explain the double recensions in the Greek and Latin respectively. Even if the book had been primitively a single composition, there must have been a dividing line in the structure which permitted the detachment of the first part with a subsequent bifurcation in its Greek textual history, as well as a separate circulation of the second part with a similar bifurcation in its Latin textual history. And if the work were not primitively a single composition, the two parts out of which the final text was compounded are probably the parts indicated by the fluctuation in the textual transmission.

We say then that the *Acta Pilati* consist of two parts, of which the first relates to the Passion and Resurrection of our Lord, and the second to the Descent into Hades: and *these two parts are respectively the Iliad and Odyssey* of the composer or composers of the Acts of Pilate.

It is strange that no one of modern critics has seen that this is the real distinction between the two parts of the composition. With the exception of Mr B. H. Cowper, I know of no one who has made this clear, and he does not seem to have followed up the clue. All that he says is that it is very apparent that this second part was appended as a sort of *Odyssey* to follow the *Iliad*[1], and that the imaginary Ananias who professes to have translated the *Acta* out of Hebrew, is altered in some copies to Aeneas, because "the name of Aeneas was very likely a conscious or unconscious imitation due to the story of Virgil of the descent of Aeneas to the underworld as found in the *Aeneid*[2]."

[1] B. H. Cowper, *The Apocryphal Gospels*, p. xciv.
[2] *Id.* p. xcii.

Mr Cowper's idea that the two parts of the Nicodemus Gospel stand to one another in the relation of *Iliad* and *Odyssey* may be re-inforced by the study of the title that we find given in a Palatine MS. to the Homeric Centones with which we have been comparing our Acts of Pilate. We have (*teste* Sylburg)[1]

Patricii Homerocentra, seu *Christiadem*, ex Iliade et Odyssea.

Now, to describe the Centones as a *Christiad* means something more than the statement that the work is a Christian work made up out of verses from the *Iliad*: it implies imitation of the method of Homer as well as the use of his language. It means that the death of Christ has replaced the death of Hector, which is the artistic goal of the *Iliad*. We shall see presently how truly this may be said, not only of the Centones, but also of the *Acta Pilati*. Either work may be described as a Christiad: the first part of the *Acta* being a Christ-Iliad, the second a Christ-Odyssey.

We will shew this conclusively by discussing the scene in which Joseph begs the body of Jesus from Pilate as described in the second recension of the *Acta Pilati* (B, xi.). We transcribe the passage, for convenience sake:

Πρὸς ἑσπέραν δὲ τῆς παρασκευῆς καταντώσης Ἰωσήφ τις ἀνὴρ εὐγενὴς καὶ πλούσιος, θεοσεβὴς Ἰουδαῖος, εὑρὼν τὸν Νικόδημον, ὃν προφθάσας ὁ λόγος ἐδήλωσε, λέγει αὐτῷ· Οἶδα ὅτι ζῶντα τὸν Ἰησοῦν ἠγάπας καὶ τοὺς λόγους αὐτοῦ ἡδέως ἤκουες, καὶ πρὸς τοὺς Ἰουδαίους εἶδόν σε μαχόμενον ὑπὲρ αὐτοῦ· εἰ δοκεῖ σοι οὖν, πορευθῶμεν πρὸς τὸν Πιλᾶτον καὶ αἰτησώμεθα τὸ σῶμα Ἰησοῦ πρὸς ταφήν, ὅτι μεγάλη ἐστὶν ἁμαρτία κεῖσθαι αὐτὸν ἄταφον. Δέδοικα, λέγει ὁ Νικόδημος, μήπως ὀργισθέντος τοῦ Πιλάτου πάθω τι κακόν· Εἰ δὲ σὺ μόνος ἀπελθὼν καὶ αἰτήσας λάβῃς τὸν τεθνηκότα, τότε κἀγὼ συνοδεύσω σοι καὶ τὰ πρὸς κηδείαν πάντα συνδιαπράξομαι. ταῦτα εἰπόντος τοῦ Νικοδήμου ὁ Ἰωσὴφ ἀτενίσας εἰς τὸν οὐρανὸν τοὺς ὀφθαλμοὺς καὶ εὐξάμενος μὴ διαμαρτῆσαι τῆς αἰτήσεως, ἀπῆλθεν πρὸς τὸν Πιλᾶτον, καὶ προσαγορεύσας ἐκαθέσθη. εἶτά φησι πρὸς αὐτόν· Δέομαί σου, κύριέ μου, εἴ τι παρὰ τὸ δοκοῦν τῇ μεγαλειότητί σου αἰτήσομαι, μὴ ὀργισθῆναί μοι· ὁ δὲ ἔφη· Καὶ τί ἐστιν ὃ αἰτεῖς; λέγει Ἰωσήφ· Ἰησοῦν τὸν ξένον, τὸν καλὸν ἄνθρωπον, ὃν ὑπὸ φθόνου οἱ Ἰουδαῖοι κατήνεγκαν

[1] Fabricius, *Bibl. Gr.* lib. ii. 7. 4.

εἰς τὸ σταυρῶσαι, τοῦτον παρακαλῶ ἵνα μοι δῷς πρὸς ταφήν. λέγει ὁ Πιλᾶτος· Καὶ τί γέγονεν ὅτι μαρτυρηθέντα τοῦτον ὑπὸ τῆς γενεᾶς αὐτοῦ ἐπὶ μαγείαις καὶ ἐν ὑποψίᾳ ὄντα λαβεῖν τὴν βασιλείαν τοῦ Καίσαρος καὶ οὕτω παρ' ἡμῶν εἰς θάνατον ἐκδοθέντα, τιμᾶσθαι αὖθις τοῦτον νεκρὸν ἐπιτρέψωμεν; ὁ δὲ Ἰωσὴφ περίλυπος γενόμενος καὶ δακρύσας τοῖς ποσὶ προσέπεσε τοῦ Πιλάτου, Μή σοι, λέγων, κύριέ μου, ἐπὶ νεκρῷ φθόνος τις ἐπιγένηται· πᾶσα γὰρ κακία ἐν τῇ τελευτῇ δεῖ συναπόλλυσθαι τοῦ ἀνθρώπου. ἐγὼ δὲ οἶδα τὴν μεγαλειότητά σου, πόσα ἐσπούδασας ὥστε μὴ σταυρῶσαι τὸν Ἰησοῦν, καὶ πόσα πρὸς Ἰουδαίους ὑπὲρ αὐτοῦ εἶπας, τὰ μὲν παραινῶν, τὰ δὲ καὶ θυμούμενος, καὶ ὕστερον πῶς τὰς χεῖρας ἀπένιψας, καὶ μηδαμῶς ἔχειν μέρος ἀπεφήνω μετὰ τῶν θελόντων ἀποκτανθῆναι αὐτόν· ἐφ' οἷς ἅπασι δέομαί σου μὴ ἀποστραφῆναι τὴν αἴτησίν μου. οὕτω τοίνυν ἐπικείμενον ἰδὼν ὁ Πιλᾶτος τὸν Ἰωσὴφ καὶ ἱκετεύοντα καὶ δακρύοντα, ἤγειρεν αὐτὸν λέγων· Ἄπιθι· χαρίζομαί σοι τὸν τοιοῦτον νεκρόν, καὶ τοῦτον λαβὼν πράττε ὅσα σὺ βουλῇ· καὶ τότε ὁ Ἰωσὴφ εὐχαριστήσας τῷ Πιλάτῳ καὶ καταφιλήσας αὐτοῦ τὰς χεῖρας καὶ τὰ ἱμάτια, ἐξῆλθεν τῇ καρδίᾳ μὲν χαίρων ὡς τοῦ ποθουμένου τυχών, τοὺς ὀφθαλμοὺς δὲ φέρων ἔτι δακρύοντας.

Now in this curious expansion of the simple statements of the Scripture, we can see that Pilate has been turned into Achilles, that Joseph is the good old Priam, begging the body of Hector, and that the whole story is based upon the dramatic passages of the twenty-fourth book of the *Iliad*.

If Joseph lifts his eyes to heaven, and prays for success in his purposed visit, it is because Priam has made similar petitions to Zeus:

> εὔχετ' ἔπειτα στὰς μέσῳ ἕρκεϊ, λεῖβε δὲ οἶνον
> οὐρανὸν εἰσανιδών, καὶ φωνήσας ἔπος ηὔδα·
> Ζεῦ πάτερ, Ἴδηθεν μεδέων, κύδιστε, μέγιστε,
> Δός μ' ἐς Ἀχιλλῆος φίλον ἐλθεῖν ἠδ' ἐλεεινόν.
>
> *Il.* Ω. 306—309.

If Joseph (quite without any suggestion to that effect from the Scriptures) will have Nicodemus to accompany him in his visit to Pilate, it is because in Homer Idaeus accompanies Priam in the expedition. But as Idaeus is left outside by Priam, the same thing is accomplished for Nicodemus in the following manner: Nicodemus expresses his fear lest Pilate should do them some harm, which is borrowed from the language of the disguised Hermes, who pretends to be afraid of Achilles:

τὸν μὲν ἐγὼ δείδοικα, καὶ αἰδέομαι περὶ κῆρι
συλεύειν, μή μοί τι κακὸν μετόπισθε γένηται.
Il. Ω. 435, 436.

The *Acta* record that Joseph enters and sits with Pilate and proffers his request; dreading refusal, Joseph falls upon his knees at Pilate's feet, and Pilate raises him and grants his petition. Whereupon Joseph kisses Pilate's hands and raiment, and departs, with tears still in his eyes, but with joy in his heart. It is but a slight modification of the Homeric account, which makes Priam embrace the knees of Achilles, and Achilles raise him and set him on a seat at his side. We may especially compare:

ἄγχι δ' ἄρα στὰς
Χερσὶν Ἀχιλλῆος λάβε γούνατα καὶ κύσε χεῖρας.
Il. Ω. 477, 478.

Τὸν καὶ λισσόμενος Πρίαμος πρὸς μῦθον ἔειπεν.
Id. 485.

Αὐτίκ' ἀπὸ θρόνου ὦρτο, γέροντα δὲ χειρὸς ἀνίστη.
Id. 515.

Ἀλλ' ἄγε δὴ κατ' ἄρ' ἕζευ ἐπὶ θρόνου, ἄλγεα δ' ἔμπης
Ἐν θυμῷ κατακεῖσθαι ἐάσομεν ἀχνύμενοί περ.
Id. 522, 523.

Surely there can be no reasonable doubt that this description of the begging of the Lord's body is cast in a Homeric mould. It may be urged that this part of the story does not appear in recension A, which has occasionally superior marks of antiquity to the alternative recension; it is, however, by no means always the case that recension A is the earlier and better text, and, even if it were, we should still have to ask what it was that prompted such Homerizing on the part of the reviser who made the other recension. Must it not have been Homer that suggested Homer? And would it not be natural to assume that it was the existence of Homeric touches in the story that prompted Homeric amplifications by scribes and editors?

The same phenomena appear when we examine the way in which the Biblical account of the wailing over the dead Christ has been expanded by the use of the narrative of the wailing of the Trojan women over Hector; and here we have the advantage of being able to shew an actual line of Homer lurking in the text of the *Acta*, and not merely the appropriation of Homeric ideas. Turning to the second recension of the *Acta* we find, in c. x., the lamentation of the Blessed Virgin and the women who were with her. The account is as follows, in curious Greek, which, it is needless to say, cannot be the primitive form, nor of early date:

ἀκούσασα ἡ θεοτόκος καὶ ἰδοῦσα αὐτὸν ὀλιγοψύχησε καὶ ἔπεσεν ἐξ ὀπίσω εἰς τὴν γῆν καὶ ἔκειτο ἱκανὴν ὥραν· καὶ αἱ γυναῖκες, ὅσαι ἠκολούθησαν αὐτῇ, ἱστάμεναι γύρωθεν αὐτῆς ἔκλαιον· ἀφ' οὗ δὲ ἀνέπνευσε καὶ ἠγέρθη, ἐβόησε φωνῇ μεγάλῃ λέγουσα· Κύριέ μου, υἱέ μου, ποῦ τὸ κάλλος ἔδυ τῆς μορφῆς σου; πῶς ὑπομενῶ θεωρεῖν σε τοιαῦτα πάσχοντα; καὶ ταῦτα λέγουσα κατέξαινε μετὰ τῶν ὀνύχων τὸ πρόσωπον αὐτῆς καὶ ἔτυπτε τὸ στῆθος· κτέ.

The lamentation is developed at much greater length in some of the MSS., as was to be expected, for the subject was one which could be expanded from tragic writers as well as from Homer. But that the sentences which we have quoted are Homeric in their origin, no one will, I think, venture to deny, for the actual line *Iliad* X. 475 is in the text: cf.

ἡ δ' ἐπεὶ οὖν ἄμπνυτο, καὶ ἐς φρένα θυμὸς ἀγέρθη
ἀμβλήδην γοόωσα μετὰ Τρῳῆσιν ἔειπεν.
Il. X. 475, 476.

The changes made are very slight; ἄμπνυτο has been replaced by the prose form ἀνέπνευσε[1], and the Homeric "gathering again of the spirits" has, by an easy confusion, been misunderstood[2] (ἠγέρθη for ἀγέρθη) so as to represent the Blessed Virgin as rising from the ground where she had fallen. Who does not see Andromache and Hecuba in the description of the wailing of Mary?

Nor is this borrowed verse the only coincidence; that the writer is here using Homer's account of the swoon of Andromache may be seen from the language of the following passage:

[1] Psellus' paraphrase of Homer helps us here; we have X. 467 Ἔπεσε δὲ ἐξ ὀπίσω· τὴν δὲ ψυχὴν ἀπέπνευσε, 475 αὕτη δὲ ἐπεὶ οὖν ἀνέπνευσε, καὶ εἰς τὴν διάνοιαν ἡ ψυχὴ ἐγένετο.

[2] Cf. the previous case suggested by us, of ἀλαλημένος taken in the sense of ἀλλόμενος.

Τὴν δὲ κατ' ὀφθαλμῶν ἐρεβεννὴ νὺξ ἐκάλυψεν,
Ἤριπε δ' ἐξοπίσω, ἀπὸ δὲ ψυχὴν ἐκάπυσσεν,

where we see the origin of the ἔπεσεν ἐξ ὀπίσω of the *Acta*. Moreover the Homeric Centones again come to our aid here, for they have a special section devoted to the *luctus sepulcrales*, and help us to determine the origin of some further details of the *Acta*[1]. A comparison shews that a great part of the lamentation in the Centones underlies the account of the *Acta Pilati*.

By the same comparison we come to suspect that the verses in which the Centonist describes the sorrow and doubt of the Virgin as she looks forward to her own future,

Πῶς ἂν ἔπειτ' ἀπὸ σεῖο, φίλον τέκος, αὖθι λιποίμην;
Πῆ γὰρ ἐγώ, φίλε τέκνον, ἴω; τεῦ δώμαθ' ἵκωμαι;

are the basis of the language of the *Acta*[2]: χωρὶς σοῦ, υἱέ μου, τί ἐγὼ γενήσομαι; πῶς ζήσω χωρίς σου; ποταπὴν βιοτὴν διάξω; (*Acta*, B, x.). But by this time it is abundantly clear, at all events as regards the first part of the composition, that the *Acta* lean on a Homeric base. And this conclusion shews us, as we have already intimated, the right way to attack the otherwise insoluble problems presented by their varying recensions and MSS.

For example, returning to the account of the paralytic, we find him relating the pain in which he lay,

κατεκείμην ἐν ὀδύνῃ πόνων.

The expression is a peculiar one, and that there has been some difficulty with it appears from the variation in the texts; for example, the Latin copies read 'in dolore pessimo,' 'in periculo et parturitione dolorum,' 'pericula plurima in parturitione dolorum'; here 'periculum' seems to have arisen from a substitution of κινδύνῳ for καὶ ἐν ὀδύνῃ: 'parturitio' is the equivalent for ὠδῖνες,

---

[1] The MSS. vary a good deal; some of them having expanded the lamentation to a great length; but even in these expansions Homer is not lost sight of; Hecuba's οἴμοι γλυκύτατε υἱέ appears frequently.

[2] From the *Acta* I suppose it passed into the Old English poem, known as the *Sowlehele*:

"So ful icham of sorwe, as any womman may beo,
That ischal my deore child in all this pyne seo;
How schal I, sone deore, how hadde I yought liuen withouten the?"

which we should naturally suspect to be a corruption of ὀδύνῃ. But on turning to Homer we find the expression which has given rise to all the trouble to be the end of a line describing the anguish of the Cyclops,

Κύκλωψ δὲ στενάχων τε καὶ ὠδίνων ὀδύνῃσι,

which at once explains the pleonasm of the Greek text, and the confusion of the Latin.

CHAPTER VI.

HOMERIC STRUCTURE OF THE DESCENSUS AD INFEROS.

WE will now demonstrate that the same phenomena are found, though in a less striking degree, in the *Descensus ad Inferos*, which we have characterized as the Christian Odyssey. It is the distinguishing religious feature of the *Odyssey* that it furnishes us with a glimpse into the state of the dead; upon two separate occasions we have the curtain drawn back from the invisible world. The first occasion is when Odysseus descends to interview Tiresias concerning the fortunes of his household and his own future. The second is when Hermes conducts to the nether world the souls of the suitors whom Odysseus has slain on his return to Ithaca. Both of these accounts furnish instructive parallels to the method of composition employed by the author of the *Descensus*. In each of the Νέκυιαι of Homer we have a succession of shades of the great dead who pass before us and give us their reminiscences of the life of the world above. The first account is in the eleventh book of the *Odyssey*; Odysseus, having gone to the far land of the Cimmerians, by the furthest ocean stream, fills a trench with the blood of slain victims, and around this trench the thirsty shades gather, and by drinking the blood acquire the power of truthful speech. First comes the shade of Elpenor, his comrade who has recently died and, being left unburied, has not yet been able to pass the gates of Hades. Then comes Tiresias the prophet, and after him the mother of Odysseus drinks the black blood and recognizes her son. This interview being ended, the story becomes a dream of Famous Women, who, in succession, tell their fortunes in life; Alkmena, Antiope and the like, mothers of heroes and demigods. Then comes a procession of the famous men, Agamemnon, Achilles and Ajax Telamon; great souls whose fellowship in the next world Homer taught

Socrates to look forward to, who would talk with him of Justice and Injustice, with personal illustrations from the 'deep damnation of their taking off.' Not very different is the procession of souls in the last book of the *Odyssey*, where again we meet with Agamemnon and Achilles.

Now let us turn to the *Descensus ad Inferos*, and examine either of its divergent Latin recensions; for the extant Greek text has not a great many marks of antiquity or originality. We find that the main idea of the writer, over and above the description of Christ's descent into Hades, is to make the dead pass in review as they do in Homer. His Christ finds, as we should naturally expect, a model in Odysseus, who descends to Hades and returns; but there are indications in the story that the writer did not merely call up in his mind a general resemblance, but that he deliberately set himself to work in Homeric parallels. Take for instance the case of Elpenor, the yet unburied comrade of Odysseus. When he appears, he is greeted with the question: 'How camest thou thither, so swift and on foot? More swiftly than I in my dark ship.' Where can we find a parallel to Elpenor in the Biblical account? Evidently the comrade in question must be the penitent thief, who might reasonably be regarded as one of our Lord's companions. It is true that there will be a slight difficulty because, in the Gospel, Christ dies before the thief. But this does not trouble our author; he sends the thief on in advance: the first recension sends him straight to Paradise to anticipate the liberated Saints from beneath; the second recension makes him knock at the barricaded doors of hell before the descending Lord. Satan opens the door a very little and lets him in. In reply to questions put to him, the thief replies; 'Ego veni praeconcitus: ipse vero post me venit continuo.'

After Elpenor we come to the prophet Tiresias; and here the suggestion was an easy one, to bring in a sequence of imprisoned prophets. It is not easy to determine what was the primitive form of the *Descensus*: but it is certain that it contained a figure that answered to Tiresias; for the first recension introduces Isaiah, as exclaiming, when the light shines in upon the prisoners: 'This is the light of which I prophesied'; he is followed by the aged Simeon and by John the Baptist, who explain their prophecies. Later on we have David as a prophet in the company. The second recension introduces Isaiah and John the Baptist with

David, as prophets who have foretold the harrowing of hell. Jeremiah is also brought in, examining his own prophecies and declaring that 'This is he of whom I prophesied to the effect that he appeared on earth and walked with men.' It must be allowed, I think, that there was an imitation of Tiresias in the original *Descensus*.

On the whole I think there is ground for saying, from the general character of the narrative, that the *Odyssey* has been imitated.

The next point is the enquiry after a possible metrical base for the story, or at least after the existence of paraphrased lines of Homer.

The language does not yield a great deal of direct coincidence with Homer, perhaps because we are further from the original document. We may begin by examining it for the conventional introductory formulae which we found employed in the first part of the *Acta*.

John the Baptist is introduced with the expression

Rec. A.   Et posthac supervenit quasi heremicola
= εἶτα ἦλθεν εἰς τὸ μέσον ἄλλος ἀπὸ τῆς ἐρήμου ἀσκητής.

Rec. B.   Tunc apparuit alius iuxta eum quasi eremicola.

Comparing with this the formula that introduces the penitent thief,

Rec. A.   Supervenit alius vir miserrimus
= ἦλθεν ἕτερος ταπεινὸς ἄνθρωπος,

we have suspicious traces of the formula used in the primitive *Acta* (Ἄλλος αὖθις πτωχὸς ἀνὴρ ἀλαλημένος ἐλθών), not only on account of the equation between the ἄλλος, ἕτερος and *alius*, and the ταπεινὸς ἄνθρωπος, πτωχὸς ἀνήρ, ἀσκητής and *vir miserrimus*, but also because we remember the substitution of such terms as μέσον σταθείς by early editors for the obscure ἀλαλημένος and compare ἦλθεν εἰς τὸ μέσον of rec. A.

Next let us see whether there is any suggestion of Calchas' formula for beginning his speech (κέλεαί με, διίφιλε, μυθήσασθαι). The *Descensus ad Inferos*, which professes to be written in the names of Leucius and Karinus, opens with a petition on the part of the writers that they may be allowed to record what they have seen: we have it in the following forms:

Greek. Κύριε Ἰησοῦ Χριστέ, ἡ ἀνάστασις καὶ ἡ ζωὴ τοῦ κόσμου, δὸς ἡμῖν χάριν ἵνα διηγησώμεθα κτέ.

Latin (A). Domine Jesu Christe, mortuorum resurrectio et vita, permitte nobis loqui mysteria etc.

Latin (B). Ego Karinus. Domine Jesu Christe, fili Dei vivi, permitte me (sic) loqui mirabilia.

That these forms are derived from the primitive Homeric line may be suspected from the second Latin recension, where the translator has adroitly, on account of the assonance, replaced διίφιλε by *Dei fili*.

Now let us return to the edited Centones and see the way in which the subject has been treated. We shall not find any special section devoted to it; but an examination of the section headed *De Centurione* will shew two versifications of the Descent into Hades embedded in the text. And in the section *De Sepultura* there is a long discourse between our Lord and Hades, who appeals to Him for mercy. The section *De Centurione* begins with the testimony of the Centurion to our Lord, continues with Christ's prayer for His murderers, and with a metrical expansion of the great Τετέλεσται of the Gospel:

Ἤδη γὰρ τετέλεστο ἅ μοι φίλος ἤθελε θυμός.

After this come the verses describing the death of the Lord and the descent into Hades, where are the Iron Gates and the Threshold of Brass:

Ψυχὴ δ' ἐκ ῥεθέων πταμένη, ἄϊδος δὲ βεβήκει
Τῆλε μαλ' ἧχι βάθιστον ἀπὸ χθονός ἐστι βάραθρον,
Τῶν ἄλλων ψυχὰς ἰδέειν κατατεθνειώτων
Ἔνθα σιδήρειαί τε πύλαι καὶ χάλκεος οὐδός,
Κάρτερος· ἔρρηξεν δὲ πύλας καὶ μακρὸν ὀχῆα.
Οἱ δ' αἰεὶ περὶ νεκρὸν ὁμίλεον ὡς ὅτε μυῖαι
Σταθμῷ ἐπὶ βρομέωσι περιγλαγέας κατὰ πέλλας
Ὥρῃ ἐν ἐαρινῇ ὅτε γλάγος ἄγγεα δεύει.

Notice the main points emphasized, the descent of the Lord, the shattering of the Gates of Hades (this is imitated from the valorous deeds of Hector in the Battle for the Ships) and the gathering of the Souls of the Dead around Him.

The Centones then return to an earlier stage of the Evangelic narrative and describe the mocking speeches addressed to our

Lord upon the Cross, and the piercing of His side with the spear. After this we have a number of lines describing the portents of nature at the Crucifixion, thunders, lightnings, earthquakes; and this leads up to the statement that the Dead became aware of what had happened, and Pluto trembled on his throne.

Ἔδδεισεν δ' ὑπένερθεν ἄναξ Ἀϊδωνεύς,
Δείσας δ' ἐκ θρόνου ἆλτο καὶ ἴαχε μάλα λιγείως.
Ὦ μοι· ἄφαρ δ' ὦιξε θύρας καὶ ἀπῶσεν ὀχῆα.
Ἦλθον ἔπειθ' ὅσα φύλλα καὶ ἄνθεα γίνεται ὥρῃ,
Ψυχαὶ ὑπὲρ ἐρέβους νεκύων κατατεθνηώτων
Ἀχνύμεναι· περὶ δ' αὐτὸν ἀγηγέραθ' ὅσσαι ἄρισται.
Ἤυσεν δὲ διαπρύσιον νεκύεσσι γεγωνώς,
Καρπαλίμως ἔρχεσθε, ἐγὼ δ' ὁδὸν ἡγεμονεύσω,
Ἔνθα κε πατρὸς ἐμοῦ τέμενος, τεθαλυῖά τ' ἀλωή.
Ὡς ἄρα φωνήσας, ἡγήσατο· τοίδ' ἄμ' ἕποντο.

Compare this account with the former and we see that it is a separate attempt at versification of the *Descensus*, but on very similar lines; we are told that great fear was caused to the lord of Hades, so that he opened the Gates and loosed the Bar (this is plainly different from the account which makes the Lord Christ break open the Gates); the gathering of the Souls in Hades is now compared with inanimate nature and not with animate; finally, the word is given, Follow me to Paradise. The two accounts are therefore slightly different.

Now it is curious that the Latin versions also shew a variety of treatment. The first account gives no mention of the breaking open of the Gates, in the second account they are shattered. The first account, after reciting the anthem of the Saints, "Aperi portas tuas ut intret rex gloriae," concludes by saying that the Lord entered "et aeternas tenebras illustravit et indissolubilia vincula disrupit," from which we naturally conclude that Hades has opened the door.

In the second account the gates and bars are smashed.

The first recension tells us that all the emancipated saints followed the Lord ("omnes sancti secuti sunt eum," with which compare ἡγήσατο· τοίδ' ἄμ' ἕποντο). The Lord then delivers them to Michael the Archangel, and all the saints follow him to Paradise ("et omnes sancti sequebantur Michaelem archangelum et introduxit eos in paradisi gratiam gloriosam"). The second recension has no mention of Paradise, but contents itself with saying, "exivimus exinde omnes cum Domino." There is not even an allusion to the entry into Paradise of the penitent thief, who has merely descended to share the common escape of the Saints.

It will be seen from the comparison that the first versification agrees most nearly with the second recension of the *Descensus* and the second versification with the first recension. It is difficult to believe that these curious relations between the documents, coupled with so many similarities in the common treatment, could have arisen unless there were some internal nexus between the Centones and the *Descensus*, and some common nucleus out of which they were all derived.

But was this nucleus metrical? The answer is that it has been shewn to be Homeric, and we have had reason in the previous pages to see how much that involves. Moreover the prose legends contain suspicious suggestions of borrowed and imitated verses. We might almost connect, without further discussion, the account of the breaking open of the doors of Hades with the line in which Hector breaks into the Greek fortification:

ἔρρηξεν δὲ πύλαν καὶ μακρὸν ὀχῆα,

if it were not that there is a somewhat similar expression in the Psalms, intimately associated with the Descent into Hades in Patristic literature, and actually referred to in one of the recensions; namely, Ps. cvi. 16 συνέτριψε πύλας χαλκᾶς καὶ μοχλοὺς σιδηροὺς συνέθλασεν. The same Psalm seems to be referred to in the first recension, where the words "tenebras illustravit et indissolubilia vincula disrupit" may be compared with ἐξήγαγεν αὐτοὺς ἐκ σκότους καὶ σκιᾶς θανάτου, καὶ τοὺς δεσμοὺς αὐτῶν διέρρηξεν (Ps. cvi. 14).

Now the reference to the Psalm does not exclude the Homeric parallel to which it would naturally lead the Centonist, but it makes it more difficult for us to say that the *Descensus* in its allusions to the bars of hell is drawing on a versified story.

Any one who reads the *Descensus* carefully will, I think, allow that there is a good deal of poetical feeling in the language; and there are not wanting cases where a parallel from Homer suggests itself readily. For example, when Hades complains of having had to disgorge Lazarus, he says that Lazarus

excutiens se ut aquila per omnem agilitatem
et celeritatem salivit exiens a nobis,

where "salivit ut aquila" is very like the Homeric

ἀλεὶς ὥς τ' αἰετὸς ὑψιπετήεις Od. ω. 538;

when the saints hear Hades and Satan quarrelling,

tunc audientes haec omnes sancti iterum
exultaverunt in gaudio,

which reminds one of

ἐγέλασσε δέ οἱ φίλον ἦτορ
γηθοσύνῃ ὅθ' ὁρᾶτο θεοὺς ἔριδι ξυνιόντας. *Il.* Φ. 389.

When Hades and Satan decide upon resistance, we have Hades addressing Satan as follows :

Si potens es praeliator, pugna adversum regem gloriae,

which is not unlike Sarpedon's advice to Glaucus,

Γλαῦκε πέπον, πολεμιστὰ μετ' ἀνδράσι, νῦν σε μάλα χρὴ
Αἰχμητήν τ' ἔμεναι καὶ θαρσαλέον πολεμιστήν. *Il.* Π. 492, 493.

Reviewing the whole of the argument in this chapter, the fact that the *Descensus* is a true *Odyssey*, the suspicious traces of the recurrence of conventional formulae employed in the Centones and in the *Acta Pilati*, the parallelism between the double versification and the double prose narration, etc., we are inclined to think that the case is made out for a primitive metrical *Descensus*; although it must be allowed that the evidence is not as striking or as conclusive as in the first part of the Nicodemus Gospel. Whether this is due to the fact that the text of the *Descensus* has gone through more hands, or to the fact that the composer worked with more liberty, is of course impossible to say.

We may now say further that, if the existence of a primitive nucleus for the Centones and the *Acta* be granted, such a nucleus must have been early: for it is on the one side the parent of all the recensions of the Centones, of which Eudocia's must be referred to the beginning of the fifth century; and on the other side it is the parent of all the recensions of the *Acta*, including the Coptic version of the 5th or 6th century, and a Latin version, of which a palimpsest exists, written in the sixth century.

Moreover there are considerations of another kind which indicate an extreme antiquity. The student of the Centones will have noticed a feature in the accounts of the miracles, the running together of separate narratives of the Gospel, without any regard to historical accuracy. Take, for instance, the treatment of the paralytic; the account in the *Acta* is clearly a combination of two cases; the one the paralytic of John v., the other from the Synoptic Gospels. But in the Centones we not only have two separate accounts of the healing of a paralytic, with distinct titles, but the separate accounts are, in all probability, compounds. For example, the second account professes to be the account of the healing of a sick man in the porch; the porch is an adaptation of the five porches of John v. But when we turn to the first account we again find that the writer has versified the detail of the sick man in the porch, by cleverly using the line

Τρητοῖς ἐν λεχέεσσιν ὑπ' αἰθούσῃ ἐριδούπῳ. *Od.* γ. 399.

But he also introduces the detail that the man was carried by his friends and laid down at the feet of the Lord, which does not belong to St John[1]. So that we may be confident that the paralytic in the primitive nucleus was a combination of sufferers.

The same thing is true of the account which is headed περὶ τοῦ χωλοῦ τοῦ καὶ ξηρὰν ἔχοντος χεῖρα, as the title, whether it be primitive or not, frankly indicates.

The blind men also are a combination; the account in the *Acta Pilati* expressly says that the man was born blind, which is from the Fourth Gospel, and that he cried, " Have mercy upon me, Son of David," which is from the Synoptics. The blind man in the Centones is a little harder to identify: possibly the statement that " he cried out the more " when reproved, underlies the verse

Ὅς τόσον αὐδήσασχ' ὅσον ἄλλοι πεντήκοντα (Mark x. 48). *Il.* E. 786.

The verses also play repeatedly on the θάρσει, with which the blind man is encouraged by the bystanders (Mark x. 49). But when we are told that the man when healed had the eyesight of an eagle,

Πάντοσε παπταίνων, ὥστ' αἰετός· ὅν ῥά τέ φασιν
Ὀξύτατον δέρκεσθαι ὑπουρανίων πετεηνῶν, *Il.* P. 674, 675;

[1] I even suspect that the story also contains a reminiscence of the cure of the leper, for the line

Αὐτὸς δ', αἴ κ' ἐθέλῃσ', ἰήσεται, οὐδέ τις ἄλλος, *Od.* ι. 520,

which occurs in both accounts in the Centones, is very Biblical.

this is merely an expansion of the statement in Mark viii. 25 καὶ ἐνέβλεπεν τηλαυγῶς ἅπαντα.

Further it is to the same chapter (viii. 26) that we owe the injunction

Νῦν δ' ἔρχευ πρὸς δῶμα, καὶ ἴσχεο, μηδ' ὀνομήνῃς· Od. λ. 251.
Μηδέ τῳ ἐκφάσθαι, μήτ' ἀνδρῶν, μήτε γυναικῶν. Od. ν. 308.

There is no doubt, then, that the section "de caeco" is a combination, though I do not see in the extant verses the allusion to ἐκ γενετῆς, which one would expect from the comparison with the account in the *Acta*. There is, however, no doubt about the method of composition.

Now let us turn to the account of the Haemorrhoousa. The writer has combined two cases of the Lord's compassion upon women, the stories of the Syrophenician and of the twelve years' flux. Accordingly he begins with

Ἔσκε δὲ πατρὸς ἑοῖο γυνὴ Φοίνισσ' ἐνὶ οἴκῳ. Od. o. 417.

There is no reason that I can see to ascribe this line to any other cause than the eclectic treatment of the writer. The case, however, is a particularly interesting one, because, as we shall see by a comparison of authorities, the Haemorrhoousa was certainly a feature of the original nucleus. And it is equally certain that in the first narration she was a double personality. We see this pretty clearly in the Centones, we can also shew it as follows for the *Acta*. Here we are told the name of the sufferer, which appears in Greek as Βερνίκη and in Latin as *Veronica*. It has commonly been supposed that the latter name was a confusion or anagram of *Vera icon*, and that it had to do with the story of the miraculous pictures of our Lord. But this is a misapprehension, as Lipsius has shewn. The name has its origin at an earlier date than any of the well-known Veronica stories. Its origin is suspected to be Gnostic, and it is the name, not primarily of the Haemorrhoousa, but of the Canaanite woman or her daughter. In the *Clementine Homilies*, for example, it is the name given to the daughter[1], probably because the writer had from some source or tradition assigned the name of Justa to the mother. The confusion between the two cases is then probably an early one.

[1] *Clem. Hom.* III. 73, IV. 1, 4, 6.

CHAPTER VII.

JUSTIN MARTYR AND THE ACTA PILATI.

WE ought next to enquire whether the previous investigations have a bearing upon certain well-known passages in Justin Martyr, in which he appears to refer to *Acts of Pilate*.

Amongst the many services which Tischendorf did to the cause of Patristic criticism, one of the greatest was the accession of new material which he brought to the study of the *Acts of Pilate*, by which he easily demonstrated the antiquity of the extant *Acta* by means of early versions dating from at least as far back as the 5th century. Whatever be the original language of the *Acta*, we find them in Latin in a Vienna palimpsest of the 5th or 6th century, and in a Coptic papyrus of at least an equal age. And it is clear that a text which we find extant and translated at so early a period must have a good claim for having existed at a much earlier period in its primitive form. Accordingly Tischendorf argued in the first edition of his *Apocryphal Gospels* that there was a continuous chain of evidence connecting the current *Acta Pilati* with the earliest times. For, according to his view, Justin Martyr quoted them in the middle of the second century, Tertullian in the beginning of the third; Maximin the Emperor circulated forged *Acts of Pilate* in the beginning of the fourth century, probably with the object of discrediting the *Acts* which were quoted by the Christians; further we have in the same century allusions to the *Acta* by Eusebius and Epiphanius; the next century brings us the testimony of Orosius; and in the sixth century we find them referred to by Gregory of Tours. But as our earliest copies belong to this period, we are, according to Tischendorf, entitled to assume the continuous existence of the

Acts of Pilate from a period earlier than that of Justin. Moreover, if this reasoning were correct there would be a strong tendency towards a belief that some at least of the non-canonical matters mentioned in the *Acta Pilati* were genuine history: and not only so, but where the account is based upon the four canonical Gospels, there is a great accession to the evidence for their currency. I suppose it was the sense of the importance of the results that would flow from the establishment of such views of the antiquity of the *Acta*, that led Tischendorf to write his tract *Pilati circa Christum judicio quid lucis afferatur ex Actis Pilati*, in which he attempted to shew that there was a probability of truth in many of the non-evangelical statements which are contained in the *Acta*. It is difficult to understand how any serious person could, after a close study of the texts, have come to any such conclusion. But it would seem that Tischendorf clung tenaciously to the belief that our published *Acts* contained nothing foreign to the second century and might therefore very well have been the *Acts* to which Justin refers; that the supposed references of Justin could be found, with sufficient nearness, in the extant texts; and that consequently the *Acts* belonged to a period in which valuable traditional information might still be current concerning the trial and death of the Lord.

Probably the best exposure of the weakness of this position will be found in R. A. Lipsius' *Critical Investigation of the Acts of Pilate*[1], and in Scholten's *Discussion of the Earliest Testimony to the New Testament Writings*[2]. Lipsius analyses the *Acta* into the following documents: first, there was the original *Acta Pilati*, which contained the first eleven chapters of the text with the omission of the prologue, and which may also have extended as far as the sixteenth chapter. It professed to be derived from a Hebrew original written by Nicodemus. Secondly, there was a *Descensus ad Inferos* current under the names of Leucius and Charinus, who are the supposed sons of Simeon who received the child Jesus into his arms; they have been permitted to return from the dead to tell the story of the Descent into Hades. Thirdly, these documents are worked over in the time of Theodosius and Valentinian in the name of a certain official named Ananias or Aeneas, to whom is

---

[1] *Die Pilatus-Acten kritisch untersucht von Prof. Dr R. A. Lipsius*, neue vermehrte Ausgabe. Kiel, 1886.

[2] Scholten, *Die altesten Zeugnisse betreffend die Schriften des neuen Testaments.*

due the first prologue to the *Acta*, the combination of the two previous writings, and perhaps the addition of chapters 12—16 of the existing *Acts*[1]. The documents thus united were worked over again at a time not earlier than the second half of the fifth century; the Latin MSS. also shew certain additional chapters which Lipsius assigns to a slightly earlier period. For the purposes of criticism, however, attention must be fixed on the first three stages of the text, which comprise the production of what we call our Christ-*Iliad* and Christ-*Odyssey*, and their combination into a single work. The main point to be noticed is that Lipsius maintains that the primitive *Acta* do not go back further than the middle of the fourth century[2].

Scholten, with whom Lipsius largely agrees, criticises the Greek of the *Acts* and the legal and other customs which are assumed in the narration, the titles of honour which are used in the address to the procurator, etc., and shews that they belong rather to the fourth century than the second. And although there are some of his criticisms that may fairly be questioned, the conclusion would seem to be very well established that the *Acta*, as we know them, betray a date at least as late as the fourth century for their period of composition[3].

---

[1] In confirmation of the detachment of these chapters it should be noticed that they are characterised by a series of striking Hebraisms, such as the following:

c. xii. ὅρον ὥρισαν.
c. xiv. ἡ φλυαρία αὕτη ἣν ἐφλυαρήσατε.
ἐκόπτοντο κοπετὸν μέγαν.
c. xv. βουλὴν κακὴν ἐβουλευσάμεθα.
λύπῃ ἐλυπήθημεν.
ἐὰν ἀκούσῃ τῶν προσταγμάτων, φυγῇ φεύγει.
c. xvi. γινώσκοντες γνώσεσθε.

Possibly these expressions may furnish the key to the self-asserted Hebrew origin of the *Acta*.

[2] *Pilatus-Acten*, p. 40. "Mag einiges in obigen als Merkmal späterer Abfassung angeführte auch erst auf Rechnung der Bearbeitung vom Jahre 425 kommen, mögen selbst die Kapitel 12—16 erst vom Bearbeiter hinzugefügt sein, so wird doch hierdurch unser oben gewonnenes Ergebniss nicht umgestossen, *das auch die Grundschrift* unserer Pilatus-Acten erst um die Mitte des 4 Jahrhunderts enstanden sei."

[3] Such contentions as those of Lipsius (*l.c.* p. 40), who finds arguments of a later date than the second century in the use of the last twelve verses of St Mark, and in the description of the temple that was forty and six years in building as Solomon's temple, may safely be set on one side. The evidence for the antiquity of the closing section of St Mark has much increased in late years, and a recent discovery by Mr Conybeare has probably found an author for it in the early part

Certainly the edited *Acta* do not belong to the second century. In their present form the preface of Ananias the Protictor couples them with the legends of the *Invention of the Cross*, which are assigned to Menander the Protictor in a Sinai MS. which I have examined; and both sets of legends agree in the feature of the insertion of Hebrew sentences disguised in Greek letters. This arouses our suspicion that in the last form of the *Acta* we have traces of an Edessene hand. But however that may be, it is very unlikely that the study of the extant *Acts* will indicate a higher date than the fourth century. But it will be asked, does this conclusion hold for the *Grundschrift*, and are the quotations of Justin to be regarded as imaginary? Let us address ourselves to these points, in order that we may see what light is thrown upon the subject by the investigations in the previous pages.

We premise that by far the major part of the arguments against the antiquity of the *Grundschrift* of the *Acta Pilati* fall to the ground at once, if that primitive writing were either wholly or in part metrical in character. We may, in dating the period of composition of the texts, make the most of late Greek and late customs involved in the Greek, but these considerations are of no weight at all against Homer. The problem of origins is entirely changed by the introduction of the idea of a poetical or semi-poetical source. The same may be said of certain confusions and misunderstandings of the Gospels which are found in the *Acta*, which are due to the license of the original writer, who is anxious to combine any Biblical features that find a Homeric echo, and is not scrupulous either in his historical treatment, nor in the actual quotations upon which he bases his story.

Moreover the problem of the chronology has much changed by the consideration that we are to find a common origin for certain parts of the Centones and of the *Acta*. On either side the analysis takes us back farther than was formerly supposed, and the common origin must claim a very respectable antiquity.

Now let us turn to the actual references in Justin to the *Acta Pilati*.

---

of the second century; and as for Solomon's temple, the same mistake which we find in the *Acta* was made in the second century by Heracleon the Gnostic. The first book of the Sibylline oracles twice calls the Temple of Herod ναὸς Σαλομώνιος (vv. 376, 393), but this part of the Oracles was, in Friedlieb's judgment, not written before the end of the second century.

There are two such references, both of them in the *First Apology*; the first is in c. 35 and runs as follows:

Καὶ γὰρ ὡς εἶπεν ὁ προφήτης, διασύροντες αὐτὸν ἐκάθισαν ἐπὶ βήματος καὶ εἶπεν· Κρῖνον ἡμῖν. τὸ δὲ "Ὤρυξάν μου χεῖρας καὶ πόδας ἐξήγησις τῶν ἐν τῷ σταυρῷ παγέντων ἐν ταῖς χερσὶ καὶ τοῖς ποσὶν ἥλων ἦν· καὶ μετὰ τὸ σταυρῶσαι αὐτὸν ἔβαλον κλῆρον ἐπὶ τὸν ἱματισμὸν αὐτοῦ, καὶ ἐμερίσαντο ἑαυτοῖς οἱ σταυρώσαντες αὐτόν· καὶ ταῦτα ὅτι γέγονεν δύνασθε μαθεῖν ἐκ τῶν ἐπὶ Ποντίου Πιλάτου γενομένων ἄκτων.

The second is in c. 48:

"Ὅτι δὲ καὶ θεραπεύσειν πάσας νόσους καὶ νεκροὺς ἀνεγερεῖν ὁ ἡμέτερος Χριστὸς προεφητεύθη, ἀκούσατε τῶν λελεγμένων. ἔστι δὲ ταῦτα· Τῇ παρουσίᾳ αὐτοῦ ἁλεῖται χωλὸς ὡς ἔλαφος, καὶ τρανὴ ἔσται γλῶσσα μογιλάλων. τυφλοὶ ἀναβλέψουσι καὶ λεπροὶ καθαρισθήσονται καὶ νεκροὶ ἀναστήσουσιν καὶ περιπατήσουσιν. "Ὅτι δὲ ταῦτα ἐποίησεν, ἐκ τῶν ἐπὶ Ποντίου Πιλάτου γενομένων ἄκτων[1] μαθεῖν δύνασθε.

To these two certain allusions to the *Acta Pilati*, a third was added by Tischendorf which is more doubtful: it is in c. 38:

Καὶ πάλιν ὅταν λέγῃ, Αὐτοὶ ἔβαλον κλῆρον ἐπὶ τὸν ἱματισμόν μου καὶ ὤρυξάν μου πόδας καὶ χεῖρας. ἐγὼ δὲ ἐκοιμήθην καὶ ὕπνωσα καὶ ἀνέστην, ὅτι κύριος ἀντελάβετό μου. Καὶ πάλιν ὅταν λέγῃ, Ἐλάλησαν ἐν χείλεσιν, ἐκίνησαν κεφαλήν, λέγοντες· Ῥυσάσθω ἑαυτόν. "Ἅτινα πάντα γέγονεν ὑπὸ τῶν Ἰουδαίων τῷ Χριστῷ, ὡς μαθεῖν δύνασθε. Σταυρωθέντος γὰρ αὐτοῦ ἐξέστρεφον τὰ χείλη καὶ ἐκίνουν τὰς κεφαλὰς λέγοντες· Ὁ νεκροὺς ἀνεγείρας ῥυσάσθω ἑαυτόν.

Here the recurrence of the phrase δύνασθε μαθεῖν, which we find in the two previous quotations, taken with the enumeration of certain things as done by the Jews to Jesus, which is precisely in the manner of the first quotation, invites the supposition that the source, from which the Roman people can get the necessary corroboration to the prophetic Scriptures, is the *Acta Pilati*.

[1] The MSS. have αὐτῶν, but the emendation of Casaubon to ἄκτων is certain, in view of the previous quotation: cf. μαθεῖν δύνασθε, which seems to be used of a written book. Justin twice refers to the writings of Moses in this way: *Apol.* i. 62 ἃ εἰ βούλεσθε μαθεῖν, ἐκ τῶν συγγραμμάτων ἐκείνου ἀκριβῶς μαθήσεσθε, and i. 63 τὰ δ' ἑπόμενα ἐξ ἐκείνων βουλόμενοι μαθεῖν δύνασθε.

Now concerning these passages and their supposed references to the *Acta*, Tischendorf says decidedly "quaecumque enim inde protulerunt veteres, quorum imprimis videndi sunt Justinus et Tertullianus, eadem in nostris inveniuntur *Actis*[1]."

Lipsius on the contrary maintains that there is no trace in our *Acts of Pilate* of the matters alluded to by Justin. The 35th chapter of the *Apology* is according to him made up as follows: κρῖνον ἡμῖν from Isaiah lviii. 2; the piercing of the hands and feet from Ps. xxi. 17; and the casting lots for the raiment from the Synoptics: not one of these details is, however, to be found in the extant *Acts of Pilate*. The 48th chapter of the *Apology* combines the prophecy of Isaiah (xxxv. 5, 6) with Matt. xi. 5; but the combination of sicknesses healed by Jesus is not found in the *Acta*, which make no mention of the healing of the dumb, and only furnish one allusion to the raising of the dead. Finally, the supposed reference in the 38th chapter of the *Apology* is a free combination of Matt. xxvii. 39 and Mark xv. 29 with a prophetic gnosis on the Passion: it is conceivable that Justin might have been thinking of some uncanonical Gospel, but with the *Acts of Pilate* the matters described have no connexion whatever.

Scholten does not believe that any *Acts of Pilate* were in the hands of either Justin or Tertullian; but that Justin merely assumed that some such official report must have been sent, and Tertullian follows Justin's assumption. In support of this view it is to be noted that Justin also refers to the returns of the Census under Quirinus, and uses the very same formula (μαθεῖν δύνασθε) as we find him employing in the case of the supposed *Acta Pilati*. Certainly he had never seen such Census papers, and he was merely assuming that some such documents must exist in the Roman archives. And it is significant that there are no quotations in Justin which we can certainly say came from the *Acta* of which he speaks.

The case, then, stands thus; either Justin's reference is wholly imaginary (which, in view of his deliberate and repeated statements, I am slow to believe), or the reference which he makes is a general one, similar in character to his allusion to the Sibyl and Hystaspes, whose writings certainly existed and were known to Justin though he does not quote them directly. The supposition,

---

[1] *Evangelia Apocrypha*, ed. ii. p. lxiii.

therefore, is invited that perhaps Justin might have alluded either to a metrical document, or to the first paraphrase of a metrical document, or to a story which was Homerized in a general sense. Such a reference is certainly possible and might have been made in perfectly good faith.

It is not however any longer a question of finding quotations from the New Testament in the *Acta*, as Tischendorf wished to convict Justin of doing: for as we ascend to the original nucleus of the *Acta*, whatever its date may be, the direct quotations disappear; and indeed one element of the, at first sight, hopeless entanglement of the later *Acts* consists in attempts which have been made to restore the Biblical expressions and sequences which were wanting in the first form of the story. We naturally should not look for Biblical quotations in a metrical account, nor in a prose account based directly on a metrical one, or Homeric in character.

Nor must we forget, in discussing the probability of the use of real *Acta Pilati* by Justin, that one reason which has been commonly assigned for dating the existence of these *Acts* and their composition at a much later period has entirely disappeared in the course of our analysis.

It has often been said that the *Acta* were fabricated in order to cover the allusions in early Christian writings: but the examination of the genesis of these Pilate legends shews them to be, in the fourth century form, not an original product, but a paraphrase of and sequence to a previously existing work. On this account, therefore, the probability is much increased that Justin really did read a book and not merely allude to a hypothetical document. Moreover it is certain that the main structure of the work to which Justin referred (if a real work be required) was exactly parallel to the composition of the existing *Acta Pilati*; viz. the miraculous cures which Jesus wrought and the sufferings which He underwent. It is a trivial criticism that would object, that we have in the *Acta* no case of healing of the dumb to answer to the prophecy of Isaiah concerning the tongue of the stammerer, or that the extant *Acta* only speak of one case of raising of the dead, or that the casting of lots for the raiment is not in the prose *Acts*. If we may judge from the Centones (with which the epigram of Patricius may be compared), the dead raised were more than a single case; and even if it be held that the supposed primitive nucleus must have been a short document, there are not wanting indications that the extant prose is in some respects an abbreviation of the primitive document [1].

Without attempting to give a final and dogmatic statement on the question, I should say that the allusions in Justin are probably from a real document, but that in any case they are allusions and not quotations. It is not impossible that he may have derived his information from a document which is a lineal ancestor of our extant *Acta*. Whether Justin, on this supposition, was deceived as to the composition of the book to which he referred, is not easy to say; if the book had already passed from a verse form into a prose paraphrase, or if it were a prose narrative affected by paraphrased lines of Homer, the illusion would readily be accounted for: but I can find any intellectual aberration credible in the case of Justin, after his blunder with regard to the Semo Sancus inscription at Rome. And we must remember that he belonged to a generation which drank down Sibyllism like water, and that Sibyllism and Homerism are, as we have shewn, first cousins.

The final settlement of the question must be left for further investigations; if our study has not been exhaustive, it may none the less furnish suggestions to those who are interested in the problems involved.

[1] The Centones have also the Casting of Lots for the raiment very well described.

CHAPTER VIII.

DIRECTIONS FOR FURTHER ENQUIRY.

WE have now reached a point at which our advance is barred, and must seek for the resolution of our difficulties by changing and extending the methods of investigation.

It may be, I think, taken for granted that we have proved (a) that there is high probability that the New Testament Scriptures were versified at a very early date, (b) that there are actual references to such versifications which go back at least into the second century. We have also shewn that the existing *Acts of Pilate* are Homerized, that Pilate is Achilles, and Joseph Priam, etc.; and that the very idea of the Descent into Hades is Homeric, and that the story itself copies the leading features of the Homeric Descents. But while we have proved this so far as to actually detect disguised lines of Homer in the existing *Acta*, we have not made a complete demonstration that all recensions of the *Acta Pilati* are alike affected by it. Nor have we been able to perfectly establish what we have stated in a suspicion, that an actual Homerized narrative of the Passion and the Descent into Hades was what Justin referred to in his enigmatical allusions to *Acts of Pilate*. We must, therefore, try to resolve the questions at issue by working on some new lines of enquiry.

Since the foregoing pages were written, Mr Conybeare has discussed in a very valuable paper the evidence which is furnished by the Armenian *Acts of Pilate*.

It is important to remark that he concedes the Homerization of the *Acta*, so far as relates to recension B of Tischendorf. But he apparently doubts the general application of the criticism, and suspects that in recension A we have very early quotations from lost Gospels, which would hardly be found in the striking form in which they occur, unless the documents which present them had drawn directly from some very early strata of Christian tradition.

We have thus to enquire whether our observed and recorded traces of Homerization in the conception and language of the *Acta* may not be a later stage in the tradition of these perplexing records. In other words we must go back to the *Acta Pilati* and find some fresh ways of interrogating them. There is great need for a fresh examination of the documents and for a fresh criticism of the text.

One direction for enquiry is that we ask whether the divergences between the existing copies and what are roughly defined as recensions may not be due in some degree to the fact of retranslation, and in particular whether there has been retranslation from a Semitic source.

The *Acts*, as we have them, affirm positively that they have been taken over from Hebrew. Thus in recension A we have the Preface of Ananias the Protictor in which he affirms that he found these *Hypomnemata* written in Hebrew, and with God's goodwill did them into Greek. The preface is usually condemned as an artifice, belonging to a late period in the propagation of the legends. The preface to recension B has something of the same kind, declaring that Nicodemus, who was a Roman toparch(!), called to him a Jew named Aeneas and besought him (ἐζήτησε) to compose a record of things which had happened. And Nicodemus himself translated the account into the Romaic dialect (by which he means Greek). The preface has a very late appearance, and yet it has some traces of being itself a translation: ἐζήτησε, for example, looks like a bad translation of the Syriac ܒܥܐ. But while we may be able to detach the prefaces and condemn them as late accretions (perhaps belonging to the same school of fabricators who are responsible for the legends of the *Invention of the Cross*), can we go so far as to say that there are no traces of Semitic hands in any part of the legends?

Now we must not adduce in evidence the existence of transcribed Hebrew phrases like

ὡσαννὰ μεμβρομῆ βαρουχαμμᾶ ἀδοναΐ,

for these are actually translated to Pilate in the document. If the document were a Hebrew one, they would not have to be translated at all; certainly they would hardly render

הושיעה בא במרומים ברוך הבא [בשם] אדוני

by the words σῶσον δή, ὁ ἐν τοῖς ὑψίστοις· εὐλογημένος ὁ ἐρχόμενος ἐν ὀνόματι κυρίου without making a ridiculous repetition. The occurrence of Hebrew words in the legends proves nothing as to the origin; it may rather be an argument against a Hebrew original.

On the other hand there are in certain chapters of recension A some remarkable Hebraisms which can hardly be artificial; for which either an explanation must be found, or allowance made.

In c. xii. we have

τῷ δὲ σαββάτῳ ὅρον ὥρισαν κτέ:

in c. xiv.

εἰς τί οὖν ἡ φλυαρία αὕτη ἣν ἐφλυαρήσατε;

and again ἐκόπτοντο κοπετὸν μέγαν:

in c. xv. οἴδαμεν ὅτι βουλὴν κακὴν ἐβουλευσάμεθα:

and to these four instances of the verb with cognate accusative we add three of the substantive verb with infinitive, viz.:

c. xv. λύπῃ ἐλυπήθημεν ὅτι ᾐτήσω τὸ σῶμα:

ἐὰν ἀκούσῃ...τῶν προσταγμάτων, φυγῇ φεύγει:

c. xvi. γινώσκοντες γνώσεσθε, οἶκος Ἰακώβ, ὅτι γέγραπται.

None of these features are found in recension B, and they all are found in chapters which may be, according to Lipsius, an accretion on the main document.

Still it should be noted that such forms occur, and an attempt should be made to find an explanation for them.

If the critical analysis of the *Acta* which has been proposed by Lipsius be trustworthy, we ought to be able to isolate the nucleus of the documents, and test them again philologically for translation or re-translation.

While we have not been able exhaustively to resolve these residual problems, we may hope that so much light has been thrown upon the documents in the course of the investigations which we have made, that it may be possible, before very long, to disentangle the history and to determine the contents of the primitive *Acta*; and there, for the present, we must leave the matter.

As for the *Centones*, a further attempt should be made to extract the nucleus from the late forms in which the verses have come down to us. We may be sure that behind Eudocia's collection there lies a shorter and rougher body of verses, for she tells us so. The question is whether we can detach Patricius' verses from Eudocia's, and whether behind Patricius we can find traces of an earlier form. There are many things in the extant Centones which suggest that the original writer was versifying a New Testament which had an early text. One such case has already been quoted in the previous pages, where we found the woman of Samaria making speeches to the people of *Sychem*. As my friend Mr McEvoy points out, this implies a text such as Jerome described which had *Sychem* for *Sychar*. And we may add that this is also the reading of the Lewis Gospels. But there are other suspicious traces of early readings. Let us examine the account of our Lord's baptism, which is a special centre for curious textual and doctrinal developments. The last four verses of the account are as follows:

Od. ι. 527 Εὔχετο χεῖρ' ὀρέγων εἰς οὐρανὸν ἀστερόεντα,
Il. Ψ. 874 Ὕψι δ' ὑπὸ νεφέων εἶδε τρήρωνα πέλειαν,
Il. Τ. 362 Αἴγλη δ' οὐρανὸν ἷκε, γέλασσε δὲ πᾶσα περὶ χθών,
Il. Φ. 382 Ἄψορρον δ' ἄρα κῦμα κατέσσυτο καλὰ ῥέεθρα.

From the third of these verses it appears that the Centonist knew the detail contained in many early Biblical texts according to which a fire was kindled in the Jordan, or, at all events, that there was some remarkable luminous appearance at the Baptism.

Another direction in which we may find a survival of early legendary matter is in the coincidences between the *Centones* and the *Infancy Gospels*. When Christ is born, we are told that his mother swaddled him and *washed him*.

Od. ψ. 325 Μήτηρ ἥ μιν ἔτικτε καὶ ἔτρεφε τυτθὸν ἐόντα,
Od. ε. 264 Εἵματά τ' ἀμφιέσατο θυώδεα καὶ λούσατο.

Two false quantities in the last line arise from the reckless borrowing of a verse in which stood the words ἀμφιέσασα and λούσασα. This can hardly be Eudocia's work, one would think, for she appears to have been both scholar and critic, and would hardly have transferred Calypso's care of her person on her farewell to Ulysses to the Blessed Virgin's care of her child in such a clumsy manner. And why this detail as to washing? Was it merely to complete the verse? Or is it not because the washing of the infant Christ is one of the favourite subjects in the *Infancy Gospels*?

We shall also find that the famous Cave of the Nativity of which the Canonical Gospels know nothing is in the Centones. The verses quoted are as follows:

Od. ε. 77 Αὐτίκ' ἄρ' εἰς εὐρὺ σπέος ἤλυθε παρθένος ἁγνή,
Il. K. 568 Φάτνῃ ἐφ' ἱππείῃ ὅθι περ μώνυχες ἵπποι
"Εστασαν.

Here again Calypso appears as the Blessed Virgin, and the Centonist has spoiled the metre of his second line by substituting for Διομήδεος, which in any case had to be got rid of, the metrically non-equivalent μώνυχες. This is not Eudocia's hand, we may be sure. And in any case, the cave is there, which is best explained by reference to the *Infancy Gospels*. Here, then, we come across suspicious traces of early readings and traditions in the Gospel. And it makes it more clear than ever that some fresh attempt should be made to disentangle from the existing Centones the original form out of which they have grown.

There is another point that requires a little attention before we take leave of our readers. It will be remembered by those who read our first studies on the text of the *Codex Bezae*, that the impulse to the enquiry after the influence of Homer on Christian doctrine and on Christian documents came to us in connexion with a curious gloss in the story of our Lord's entombment, which we suspected to be metrical, and to be taken from a Latin Homerizer or Centonist. Something similar had been half suspected by Scrivener, who, in speaking of the 'stone which twenty men could hardly lift,' said that 'it was conceived somewhat in the Homeric spirit.'

Since we wrote our chapter on the traces of the Latin Centonist in the *Codex Bezae*, the whole problem of the genesis of the New Testament text has been reflected in the discussion of the origin of this gloss. Dr Chase claimed it as a convincing case of retranslation from the Syriac, and brought forward an illustration from Josephus in which similar language was used of the opening of the doors of the temple, together with what one can only describe as a little sermon on the analogies between the temple at Jerusalem and the tomb in which our Lord was laid. On the other hand, Dr Blass has vigorously defended the passage as a genuine Lucan fragment preserved in the Roman recension of the Gospel. In his recent work *The Philology of the Gospels*, he suggests a Greek original for the supposed gloss, in preference to my imagined Latin, thus taking us right back to *Odyssey* ix. 240 without the mediation of a Centonist. Naturally the existence of the latter would have been fatal to his theory that the sentence was due to Luke himself. According to Blass, then, we are to look for the key in the words of Homer:

Αὐτὰρ ἔπειτ᾽ ἐπέθηκε θυρεὸν μέγαν ὑψόσ᾽ ἀείρας,
Ὄβριμον· οὐκ ἂν τόν γε δύω καὶ εἴκοσ᾽ ἄμαξαι
Ἐσθλαὶ τετράκυκλοι ἀπ᾽ οὔδεος ὀχλίσσειαν.

Here, says Blass, you have the verb ἐπέθηκεν used in Luke [rec. β] while Matthew and Mark use προσκυλίω. He then makes apologies (which are quite unnecessary) for the quotation of Homer by the learned physician. So it seems as if the whole question of the New Testament text is involved in the story of this single gloss.

We do not propose to decide the question or questions involved, at the present stage of the enquiry: but we will add some fresh material for the study of the passage (whether it be a gloss or an original fragment of St Luke).

For it appears that such big stones described in similar Homeric or quasi-Homeric language turn up much more frequently than would have been suspected.

We have to begin with the parallel adduced by Dr Chase from Josephus (*B. J.* VI. 5. 3)

ἡ δὲ ἀνατολικὴ πύλη τοῦ ἐνδοτέρου, χαλκῆ μὲν οὖσα καὶ στιβαρωτάτη, κλειομένη δὲ περὶ δείλην μόλις ὑπ᾽ ἀνδρῶν εἴκοσι...ὤφθη κατὰ νυκτὸς ὥραν ἕκτην αὐτομάτως ἠνεῳγμένη.

The big stone also turns up in the Koran c. 28, where we have an instructive note of Sale's, taken from the Moslem commentators:

> So [Moses] watered [their sheep] by rolling away a stone of prodigious weight which had been laid over the mouth of the well by the shepherds and required no less than seven men (though some name a much larger number) to remove it.

The Midrash upon the size of the stone which Moses removed cannot have been invented by the commentators upon the Koran. They probably got it from Jewish writers.

Turning to Aphrahat (IV. 6) we find him saying of the stone which covers the well in Gen. xxix., which *Jacob* rolls away, that it was so heavy that 'many shepherds were not able to take it away so as to open the well until Jacob came.' And St Ephrem also, in his commentary on Genesis, has a remark on the size of the stone which Jacob removed from the well:

ܗܕܐ ܕܝܢ ܐܢܘܢ ܩܕܡܝܗ. ܒܕܒܪܐ ܕܒܐܠܗܐ. ܒܗ ܗܘܐ ܗܘܐ ܒܗ. ܠܐܦܐ ܣܓܝܐܬܐ ܕܠܓܒܪܐ ܣܓܝܐܐ ܗܘܘ ܠܗ.

i.e. he accomplished this triumph before her (sc. Rachel) in that, by means of the Son who was hidden within him, he rolled away the stone which very many men could hardly lift.

The great stone moved by Jacob is also commented on by Cyril of Alexandria (*Glaph.*, P. G. 69, 167):

δυσαχθὴς μὲν γὰρ τῷ φρέατι λίθος ἐπέκειτο ὃν πλείστη μὲν ὅση ποιμένων ἄθροισις ἀπεσάλευε μόλις· ἕδρα δὲ τοῦτο καὶ μόνος ὁ Ἰακώβ.

It appears, then, as a conventional Midrashic element in the Old Testament, both in Genesis and in Exodus. A somewhat similar instance will be found in the Christian martyrology (*Acts of S. Nereus and S. Achilles*):

οὐ μὴν ἀλλὰ καὶ ἑκάτερον βαρύτερον λίθον, ὃν ἕβδομοι ἄνδρες μετὰ βίας ἐκούφιζον, εἰς τὸν ὦμον αὐτοῦ ἐπιθέντος, αὐτὸς ἐπὶ δύο μίλια ὥσπερ ἐλαφρὰ ἄχυρα ἐβάσταζεν καὶ ἐν αὐτῷ τῷ τόπῳ ἔθετο ἐν ᾧ εὔξασθαι εἰώθει.

The last two passages are at least valuable for the clearing of one point. In the *Codex Bezae*, we had what seemed an unnatural construction in the Greek in the words λείθον ὃν μόγις εἴκοσι ἐκύλιον. There is no need to resort to retranslation from the Syriac to justify the use of the imperfect, when we have a similar usage both in Cyril and in the *Acts of Nereus and Achilles*.

DIRECTIONS FOR FURTHER ENQUIRY.

Here, then, is a modest increment of parallels for the discussion of the Bezan gloss.

There are plenty of big stones to be found that they may be placed side by side with that of Joseph of Arimathea; and the Biblical commentators and writers of Midrash keep a stock of them. It would be presumptuous to say that they are all Homeric. Yet the parallels with Homer are often so close that we can hardly help suspecting that some of them came from the cave of the Cyclops. But whether the particular one, whose dimensions are regarded as phenomenal in the *Codex Bezae*, belongs to that group which Homer has set rolling, is still an open question. And of the whole problem presented by the gloss, we can only say at present in biblical language, that it is 'a burdensome stone for all peoples,' and in quasi-biblical terms that 'twenty critics have not yet succeeded in moving it.'

www.ingramcontent.com/pod-product-compliance
Lightning Source LLC
Chambersburg PA
CBHW070325100426
42743CB00011B/2559